GREAT MEDITERRANEAN PASSENGER SHIPS

WILLIAM H. MILLER

The
History
Press

The 1960s was a high point in Italian ocean liner creation and construction, and this included the *Michelangelo*, seen here whilst being built at Genoa in 1964. (Maurizio Eliseo Collection)

First published 2016

The History Press
The Mill, Brimscombe Port
Stroud, Gloucestershire, GL5 2QG
www.thehistorypress.co.uk

British Library Cataloguing in Publication Data.
A catalogue record for this book is available from the British Library.

ISBN 978 0 7509 6308 4
Typesetting and origination by The History Press
Printed in China

Cover paintings by Stephen Card: *front*: *Olympia*; *rear*: *Raffaello*.

CONTENTS

ACKNOWLEDGEMENTS

Like the officers and crew of a passenger ship, it takes many hands to assemble a book – the photographs, anecdotes, the cover art. The title is no exception.

First of all, my great thanks to The History Press and Amy Rigg for taking on this project. Thanks also to Stephen Card for his superb cover art, to Dieter Killinger for his evocative Foreword and to Michael Hadgis for his technical assistance.

Further appreciation to Captain Nicola Arena, Scott Baty, Marion Carlson, Tom Cassidy, Len Chapman, Captain Dimitrios Chilas, Anthony Cooke, Luís Miguel Correia, the late Alex Duncan, Maurizio Eliseo, Richard Faber, John Ferguson, Captain Narciso Fossati, William Fox, Ugo Frangini, the late Alex Garcia, Captain Raffaelle Gavino, Alan Goldfinger, Charlotte Green, Eric Johnson, Andrew Kilk, Norman Knebel, Peter Knego, Anthony La Forgia, Captain James McNamara, Sue Mauger, Gregory Maxwell, Tim Noble, John Palermo, Robert Pelletier, Paolo Piccione, Captain Paolo Piovino, Tony Ralph, Rino Rivieccio, Giancarlo Roccatagliata, Sal Scannella, the late Antonio Scrimali, Lawton Thomas, the late Captain Mario Vespa, Steffen Weirauch, James Wheeler and Albert Wilhelmi.

Organisations that have assisted include Companhia Colonial de Navegação, Costa Cruises, Greek Line, Italian Line, MSC Cruises, Moran Towing & Transportation Company, Port Authority of New York & New Jersey, Steamship Historical Society of America, World Ocean & Cruise Liner Society, World Ship Society and Zim Lines.

FOREWORD

Working for the Italian Line at the New York office in the mid 1960s was without doubt the highlight of my long career in travel. To get up in the morning and know that you were going to enjoy each day to the fullest felt like play as opposed to a mundane day-to-day job. To be assistant sales manager for the Italian Line at a time when such great liners as the *Michelangelo* and *Raffaello* made their debuts was a thrilling and once-in-a-lifetime experience. Sailing up the Hudson River on maiden voyage arrival days was something to cherish all my life.

As part of my duties, I interviewed passengers in three classes – first, cabin and tourist – and on sailing days I visited and saw off VIP passengers such as Joan Crawford, Arturo Toscanini and other luminaries. I shall never forget the beautiful liners of the Italian Line – the sister ships *Michelangelo* and *Raffaello*, the graceful *Leonardo da Vinci* and the elegant but smaller *Cristoforo Colombo*. Each ship was a classic beauty, the likes of which we will not see again.

I was very lucky to have experienced this special time. In the following pages of Bill Miller's *Great Mediterranean Passenger Ships*, I wish you the best of luck on this fascinating passage through steamship history.

Dieter Killinger
New York City, Summer 2015

Dieter Killinger is a long-time friend of the author and has long been employed in the travel industry, including periods with the Italian Line, North German Lloyd, American Export Isbrandtsen Lines and Society Expeditions.

INTRODUCTION

When thinking of Mediterranean passenger liners, I think of a romantic version: summer-like, mild-weather voyages, bright sunshine and deep blue waters, and lido deck swimming pools with clusters of umbrellas filled with sunbathing passengers. I look back to the 1950s and '60s mostly, to those final times before speedy, if less graceful, and charismatic airliners took hold and dominance. Those times created a vast and diverse collection of passenger ships, flying the flags of the likes of Italy, Spain, Portugal, Greece and, more unusually for passenger shipping, Egypt and Turkey. And what a collection of ships – from the big liner fleet of, say, the Italian Line to the small, converted ex-Victory ships such as Egypt's *Khedive Ismail* and *Mohammed Ali El Kebir*. But clearly, there are far too many Mediterranean passenger ships to include in a book of this size. Consequently, I have to make considerable cuts – instead selecting only some of the ships. Hopefully, this book will succeed as an overview.

Creating this book, gathering the quotes and anecdotes and added reflections has been a great pleasure. It has added to my own understanding of these Mediterranean passenger ships and has brought back many fine and happy memories. These include voyages on such ships as the *Homeric, Queen Frederica, Cristoforo Colombo, Amerikanis* and *Ellinis*. More specifically, I recall crossing on the *Raffaello* in the summer of 1973 from Naples to New York, a ten-day passage that was part of a so-called 'Mediterranean go-round' cruise as well. We had full-day calls at Genoa, Cannes, Barcelona, Gibraltar/ Algeciras and finally Lisbon. Passengers still 'shared' on crossings and it was $600 for a berth in a cabin-class double. The other passengers were often very interesting and usually well travelled, the service still very good and the pasta flawless. Moored off Cannes, I especially recall the barge-tender coming alongside and then offloading some mighty Cadillac and Rolls-Royce automobiles into the forward holds and later some of those brown, well-labelled Vuitton trunks. That night, there were gala fireworks sponsored as a goodwill gift by the Chinese government. The 902ft-long *Raffaello* sat, with almost all of her external lights switched off, as multi-coloured splashes and sprays of mixed colours soared around her. More than a week later, when we finally reached Pier 86 at New York, the *Michelangelo* arrived an hour before us. She was inbound from an August cruise to the Caribbean. This great $120-million pair of mighty Italians – then the ultimate Mediterranean liners – were together at New York on what was a rare occasion.

These pages are filled with nostalgia, history, information and, like me, with some memories. It is a bright, sun-drenched summer morning. A passenger liner, perhaps white hulled, berthed, or possibly arriving, in a southern European port. The whistles are sounding, passengers wave farewell, flags flutter at the mastheads and the *Raffaello*, let's say, is departing from Genoa.

Bill Miller
New Jersey, USA

1

PASSING GIBRALTAR:
PRE-WAR LINERS FROM THE MEDITERRANEAN

Rex & Conte di Savoia

As something of a beginning, I looked back to 1932. It was indeed a banner year for the Mediterranean, especially for the Italians. With the full support and encouragement of the Mussolini government, the principal Atlantic liner companies were merged as the more effective, more appropriate and hopefully more profitable Italian Line. It also meant that two of the world's largest and grandest liners were introduced – the 51,000-ton *Rex* that September and then the 48,500-ton *Conte di Savoia* two months later in November. And just the year before, one of the finest and fastest liners ever built for Europe–Far East service, the 13,000-ton *Victoria* of Lloyd Triestino, had been commissioned. The Italians greatly dominated among all Mediterranean liners then, with such other liners as the *Augustus* and *Roma*, *Conte Biancamano* and *Conte Grande*, *Saturnia* and *Vulcania*, *Duilio* and *Giulio Cesare*, *Conte Rosso* and *Conte Verde*, and some smaller passenger ships as well.

Sadly, many of these ships were destroyed during the Second World War. The Italian passenger fleet was all but in ruins by the end of the war. In this book, coverage begins in the late 1940s, at a point when the Italian Line began to be rebuilt while other Mediterranean passenger ship fleets were expanding or developing anew.

The splendid *Rex* at sea. (ALF Collection)

Summer morning: the 880ft-long *Rex* anchored off Villefranche. (ALF Collection)

Joyous reception: docking at New York's Pier 88 during her first arrival in September 1932. (ALF Collection)

Festive occasion: the 2,200-passenger *Conte di Savoia* departing from Genoa on her maiden crossing to New York in November 1932. (ALF Collection)

Liners together: the 48,502grt *Conte di Savoia* berthed at Genoa with the *Conte Grande* and *Duilio* to the left. (ALF Collection)

Luxury at sea: the first-class ballroom aboard the *Rex*. (Author's Collection)

With their pools and lido decks, the likes of the *Rex* were dubbed the 'Rivieras afloat'. (Italian Line)

Speed queen to the Far East: the superb *Victoria* of Lloyd Triestino at Venice. (Lloyd Triestino)

2

POST WAR: REBIRTH OF THE ITALIANS

Italian Line: *Saturnia* & *Vulcania* and *Conte Biancamano* & *Conte Grande*

As we sipped drinks in his lavish, richly appointed office-dayroom aboard the 70,000grt Carnival cruise liner *Sensation* during a voyage from Miami to the Caribbean in 2000, Captain Raffaelle Gavino reminisced about his time at sea. His thoughts turned to earlier days at sea, especially the ones with the once famous and popular Italian Line, Italy's premier passenger ship company. The captain, who was then on the eve of his 70th birthday, never paused to recall a ship, a port or even an exact date. He had an exceptional memory for detail; his mind was encyclopaedic.

Both Captain Gavino's grandfather and father had been seamen. His father actually served with the Italian Line in the 1930s, sailing aboard such liners as the *Conte Grande* and *Conte Biancamano*. The young Gavino followed in the family footsteps and attended the naval college in the family's home town of Genoa. He too had hoped to join the Italian Line, but by the time of his graduation in 1946, the company's fleet was hugely diminished. He had to wait a year, during which he served in very small coastal cargo vessels, before becoming a cadet on an Italian Line Liberty ship, the 7,200grt *Tritone*.

His first passenger ship came a few years later, in the early 1950s, when he joined the combo liner *Ugolino Vivaldi*, a 9,800grt combination passenger-cargo ship then sailing on the Italy–Suez–Australia migrant and freight run. The *Vivaldi* was one of six sisters. Ordered in 1940, just as the war was to start for the Italians, these six freighters were intended for South American service. At best, however, construction was sluggish. Three were launched in 1942; the other three just as the war ended in 1945. Planned to each have twelve-passenger berths, they were fitted out with expanded superstructures and accommodations. They were completed with beds for ninety in cabin class and 530 in dormitory-style third class.

The first trio were launched as the *Paolo Toscanelli*, *Ferruccio Buonapace* and *Mario Visentini*. But there were changes prior to completion – the *Buonapace*

Restored after the war, the 23,970grt *Vulcania* at sea, en route to New York. (Italian Line)

became the *Ugolino Vivaldi* and the *Visentini* changed to *Sebastiano Caboto*. The second set of three sisters was finally completed in 1948–49. These 9,700-ton ships were named *Marco Polo*, *Amerigo Vespucci* and *Antoniotto Usodimare*. They were rerouted upon completion to the west coast of South America service – from Naples, Genoa, Cannes, Barcelona and Tenerife to La Guaira, Curaçao, Cartagena, Cristóbal, the Panama Canal, Buenaventura, Puna, Callao, Arica, Antofagasta and finally Valparaíso. Genoa all the way to Valparaíso took thirty days and so sailings from Italy were just about monthly.

Almost immediately, however, the six ships were surplus to trading requirements. Consequently, two of the earlier ships, the *Sebastiano Caboto* and *Ugolino Vivaldi*, were chartered to Lloyd Triestino and refitted for its Italy–Australia service. Both were returned to the Italian Line in 1951 for further South American sailings.

The *Saturnia* had a slightly different funnel from the *Vulcania* but otherwise they were very similar ships. (Eric Johnson Collection)

Sailing day for the *Vulcania*. it was a two-week journey to New York from Trieste and Venice. (Italian Line)

'Aboard the 485ft-long *Vivaldi* we carried ninety-five passengers in first class, in comfortable cabins,' recalled Captain Gavino, who sailed during the Lloyd Triestino charter:

> 735 in steerage, in third class, in dormitories erected in cargo holds. The ship was full on every trip going out to Fremantle, Melbourne and Sydney. The steerage passengers were mostly Italians, but we also had some French, German, Yugoslavian and Greek migrants. Many had free tickets that were provided in return for five years of work in Australia before they could return free.

In 1958, three of these ships were downgraded to freighters – the other three in 1963. Except for the *Paolo Toscanelli*, which was mechanically troubled and scrapped in 1973, they endured until 1978, when the rest also went to the breakers.

The Italian merchant marine was in ruins following the Second World War. Almost all large passenger ships were either lost or in Allied hands. These included four of the nation's largest liners – the *Saturnia*, *Vulcania*, *Conte Biancamano* and *Conte Grande* – which were with the Americans. Eventually, they would be returned and restored. Built in 1927 at Monfalcone, the *Saturnia* – which was used during the latter part of the Second World War as the US hospital ship *Frances Y. Slanger* – weighed in at 24,346 tons in the late 1940s. Her near but not identical sister the *Vulcania* was completed a year later, in 1928.

Once regular transatlantic service – between Naples, Genoa, Cannes, Gibraltar and New York (there was a westbound call at Halifax as well) –

Fun at sea: deck games aboard the *Saturnia* in the 1950s. (Italian Line)

of the first class staterooms, which I think were larger than ordinary cabins, had private verandas, a sort of balcony, the kind we find on cruise ships of today. The Italian staff members were very courteous, very charming, very efficient and very friendly to regular passengers. All-Italian crews, they seemed to have great pride in their work, in their ship, in Italy itself. Many had worked on the big Italian liners from before the Second World War, ships like the *Rex* and the *Conte di Savoia*.

was revived in 1948–49 the Italian Line was once again a very popular company. The business and tourist trades in first and cabin class resumed while migration slowly increased, filling westbound tourist-class berths.

'When I was 6, in 1949, we went to Italy on the *Saturnia*. We sailed to Naples. My father had business interests in Rome and it was the first of many trips for me in those wonderful Italian Line ships,' remembered John Palermo. 'There weren't many tourists in first class back then. It was mostly business people and government officials and the high Catholic clergy, bishops and archbishops.' He added, 'We returned to the States on the *Vulcania*, which was almost a twin to the *Saturnia*.' The 19-knot motor liner had accommodations for 232 first-class, 262 cabin-class and 862 tourist-class passengers.

Palermo remembers:

The *Saturnia* and *Vulcania* had very ornate interiors which, as I recall from later visits, were really heavy and dark and actually unlike the sleek, very contemporary Italian-Mediterranean styles of the 1950s and afterward. There was a very small top-deck pool and lido area, where the ship's staff organised games and other fun activities. Sitting on a long pole and then being knocked off and into the pool was one of them. There were children's activities as well and a special tea party in the afternoon and even separate meals for kids. Many

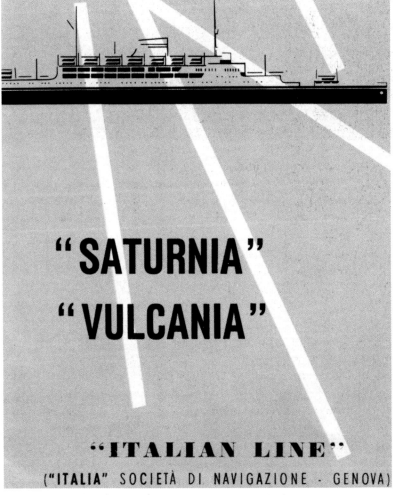

"SATURNIA"

"VULCANIA"

"ITALIAN LINE"

("ITALIA" SOCIETÀ DI NAVIGAZIONE - GENOVA)

A 1950s promotional brochure. (Author's Collection)

Captain Raffaelle Gavino served aboard the stately *Vulcania* in the early 1950s: 'An older, very ornate ship, she was actually a "castle-at-sea" with wood carvings, polished mahogany, a vestibule and grand stairwell, and a first-class restaurant that was two decks high.'

The two ships were retired from Italian Line service in the spring of 1965, just as the brand-new *Michelangelo* and *Raffaello* were due to be commissioned. The *Saturnia* was scrapped later that same year at La Spezia. The *Vulcania* was sold to Grimaldi-Siosa Lines, becoming their *Caribia* and running the Europe–West Indies service and later Mediterranean cruising. She grounded in windy conditions off Cannes in September 1972 and was badly damaged. Too old for major repairs, she was later refloated, patched up at Genoa and then sold to Italian shipbreakers at La Spezia. They resold the 44-year-old ship to breakers at Barcelona, who in turn resold her to Taiwanese scrap merchants, who had her towed out to the Far East. In July 1974, while awaiting a berth at Kaohsiung, the old ship sprang leaks and began flooding. She was later pumped out and then brought into port to finally meet the demolition crews.

A dramatic aerial view at Naples: the *Saturnia* is in the foreground; the *Andrea Doria* (left) and *Cristoforo Colombo* are berthed at the outer end; and American Export Lines' *Excalibur* is at the far left. (ALF Collection)

A winter Mediterranean cruise aboard the *Vulcania*. (Author's Collection)

Also near-sisters, the *Conte Biancamano* and *Conte Grande* were both restored for their Italian owners after the war. The Glasgow-built *Conte Biancamano* was commissioned in 1925 while the Italian-constructed *Conte Grande* made her first debut three years later. They were used on the Italy–New York and South American runs, and later were used in Lloyd Triestino's service out to the Far East. Laid up at Santos after Italy entered the war in Europe in the spring of 1940, the *Conte Grande* was seized a year later by the Brazilian government, but then promptly resold to the US government, becoming the trooper USS *Monticello*. The *Conte Biancamano* was laid up at Cristóbal in Panama in early 1940 and then she too went to the Americans in December 1941. She became the USS *Hermitage*. Both ships gave heroic service until returned to Italy in 1947. Unlike the *Saturnia* and *Vulcania*, the *Conte Biancamano* and *Conte Grande* underwent two-year refits and modernisations. The *Biancamano* was actually lengthened by 12ft and fitted with a more modern bow. The *Conte Grande* was lengthened as well, but was also given new, wider funnels.

While suited primarily to the post-war tourist and migrant trades, their berthing arrangements included the still traditional three classes. The 23,842-ton *Conte Biancamano*, for example, carried 1,578 passengers in her post-war guise – 215 in first class, 333 in cabin class and 1,030 in tourist.

Crowds gather to see the departure of the newly restored post-war *Conte Biancamano* in 1949. (Italian Line)

Late afternoon at Genoa: the *Conte Biancamano* is on the left, the *Cristoforo Colombo* to the right. (Richard Faber Collection)

A dormitory in third class aboard the post-war *Conte Biancamano*. (Paolo Piccione Collection)

Three liners in port at Naples: Orient Line's *Oronsay* is on the left, the *Conte Grande* in centre position and the *Vulcania* to the right. (Italian Line)

Being among the most lavishly ornate and stylised of pre-war liners, their post-war interiors were changed drastically. They were often said to be the first contemporary large Italian liners, featuring the sleek, modern decor that would go into the likes of the 1951–52-built *Augustus* and *Giulio Cesare* and then the *Andrea Doria* and *Cristoforo Colombo* of 1952–54. 'In the 1950s, we crossed on the *Conte Biancamano*, *Augustus*, *Cristoforo Colombo* and, my favourite of all, the *Leonardo da Vinci*,' said Palermo:

Sadly, we never made trips on the *Andrea Doria* or the last two Italian liners, the *Michelangelo* and *Raffaello*. I remember that the *Conte Biancamano* looked old on the outside with two lean stacks and lots of ventilators, but had been greatly modernised, updated, on the inside. After the War, and then her refurbishing, she hinted at the stylish, very contemporary, almost sleek decor that became the signature of the Italian Line at that time. Uniquely, I seem to remember the *Biancamano* had a pool placed between her two stacks. The *Conte Grande* did too, but I think they were the only two ships then afloat with such a feature.

Lloyd Triestino's *Australia* is on the left, the *Conte Grande* on the right. The third passenger ship is not identified. (ALF Collection)

In her post-war guise, the 652ft-long *Conte Grande* was a very handsome-looking liner. (Italian Line)

A busy day at Genoa: from left to right: Sitmar's *Castel Bianco*, Union Castle's *Dunnottar Castle*, then *Andrea Doria*, *Cristoforo Colombo* and, departing, the *Conte Grande*. (Italian Line)

Resuming service in 1949, the *Conte Biancamano* and *Conte Grande* were used in the full resumption of Italian Line's South American service – from Naples, Genoa, Cannes, Barcelona, Lisbon and Dakar to Rio de Janeiro, Santos, Montevideo and Buenos Aires. In peak summers, the *Conte Biancamano* was used on the New York run; the *Conte Grande* helped also, but only for two voyages in 1956 following the loss of the *Andrea Doria*.

These two liners had long, busy and popular lives, but grew tired by the late 1950s. The *Conte Biancamano* was laid up in April 1960 and sold to scrappers at La Spezia four months later. The *Conte Grande* was demolished a year later.

Italian Line: *Giulio Cesare & Augustus*

'The *Augustus* and *Giulio Cesare* were unusually big motor liners for their time, at 27,000 tons each. Fiat had very special interest in both of them,' remembered Captain Fossati, who served aboard both:

Fiat technicians and engineers actually inspected each ship following every round voyage. Their diesels were built just before World War Two, in 1939, but kept in storage until the early '50s. When the plans for these ships were first drawn in 1948, someone remembered the diesels. They were a perfect choice as well as being a post-war showcase for Italian propulsion systems. Actually, they were the largest Fiat diesels yet fitted to a ship. The 680ft-long *Augustus*

as well as the *Giulio Cesare* were built with post-war American financial help, through the Marshall Plan.

Captain Raffaelle Gavino was third and then second mate on board the likes of the *Giulio Cesare*, *Cristoforo Colombo* and *Vulcania*: 'The *Giulio Cesare* was new and very modern, and a very beautiful-looking vessel. She carried lots of migrants going to South America, to Brazil, Uruguay and Argentina.'

C.M. Squarey, the noted British passenger ship observer, made a short trip aboard the *Giulio Cesare* in March 1952. He later wrote, 'The Italians are masters at the art of shipbuilding as well as masters of the art of hotel-keeping, and this fine vessel is no exception.' Mr Squarey wrote further:

The *Giulio Cesare* is a smart ship in every way, but perhaps the greatest progress of all has been made in her third-class quarters [capacity 776] where the cabins as well as the public rooms would seem like a dream to many a humble emigrant. The cabins are 2-, 4- and 6-berth, all with hot and cold running water and even reading lamps over every berth. There is a splendid main lounge and smoke room and bar whilst the dining saloon is of impressive proportion and nicely furnished. There are even some tables for two in it! This class even has its own permanent, mosaic-tiled swimming pool.

The 1952-built *Augustus* was 'wonderfully modern' according to passenger John Palermo:

Glorious trio: from left to right: *Federico C*, *Augustus* and *Cristoforo Colombo*. (ALF Collection)

The splendid-looking, 27,078grt *Giulio Cesare* arriving at Boston's Commonwealth Pier. (Italian Line)

1950s Italian style: first class aboard the *Augustus*. (Italian Line)

She had large public rooms, wider decks and a swimming pool and surrounding lido for each class – first, cabin and tourist. And all the staterooms even in cabin class had a private shower and toilet. My family did a trip on the *Augustus* in 1957 just after she was brought over from the South American service, between Genoa and Rio de Janeiro and Buenos Aires, to help out on the North Atlantic, assisting with the high demand on the New York run. The *Andrea Doria* had sunk the year before, in July 1956, and so the Italian Line was short of berths, especially in the busy summer season.

According to Captain Fossati, 'These ships actually earned a double profit for some years – Latin America sailings in the peak winter [summer in the southern hemisphere] and then New York in the equally busy northern summer.'

The *Giulio Cesare* had developed mechanical as well as rudder troubles in 1972. She was quickly deemed unworthy of costly repairs and subsequently the 21-year-old liner was sold to scrappers at La Spezia. The *Augustus* was not retired until the winter of 1976. She evaded the scrap merchants, however, and found further life out in Far Eastern waters (see Chapter 12).

Finished with engines: the *Giulio Cesare* being scrapped at La Spezia in 1973. (Antonio Scrimali)

The *Augustus* departing from New York in June 1957, with the *Gripsholm, Queen of Bermuda* and *Ocean Monarch* docked in the background. (Moran Towing & Transportation Co.)

3

GRAND RENAISSANCE

Italian Line: *Andrea Doria* & *Cristoforo Colombo*

Captain Raffaelle Gavino was serving aboard the *Augustus*, sailing off West Africa north of Dakar and bound for South America, on that tragic date in Italian maritime history, 26 July 1956:

> I was second mate on watch in the bridge when the captain arrived to tell us that the *Andrea Doria* had been in a serious collision off the coast of New England and that she was in great danger. But we were assured that she was slowly headed for the coast to be grounded. But a few hours later, the captain returned and gave us the very sad news. The *Andrea Doria* had sunk. It was very, very emotional. We later advised the passengers and crew aboard the *Augustus*. Many cried.

Constructed by Ansaldo Shipyards at Genoa, the *Andrea Doria* was 29,083grt, 700ft in length and could make 23 knots with her steam turbine, twin-screw

The *Cristoforo Colombo* fitting out at Genoa in a photograph dated 7 March 1954. (Italian Line)

A view at Genoa: Adriatica Line's *Enotria* is on the left, the *Conte Biancamano* in the centre and the *Cristoforo Colombo* on the right. (Italian Line)

Preparing for her maiden crossing to New York, the 700ft long *Cristoforo Colombo* takes a quick turn in dry dock at Genoa in a photo dated 20 July 1954. (Italian Line)

The 1,055-passenger *Cristoforo Colombo* arriving on her maiden call at Boston. (ALF Collection)

propulsion. She had accommodations for 1,241 passengers: 218 first class, 320 cabin class and 703 tourist class.

'The *Cristoforo Colombo* had a special place in the Italian Line fleet after the *Doria*, her sister ship, went down,' remembered John Palermo:

The *Colombo* was, at least temporarily, the national flagship, the largest, fastest and finest liner under the Italian flag. We did several trips aboard her. It was eight days to Naples with a quick stop at Gibraltar. Homeward to New York, it took a little longer as we sailed up to Genoa and Cannes before revisiting Gibraltar and then crossing the mid Atlantic. I remember Pier 84 very well too. It was the Italian Line's terminal at the foot of West 44th Street in New York. In those days, every Manhattan taxi cab driver knew the piers, their location and the shipping lines that used them. It was interesting that once, during one of those crippling Italian seamen's strikes, we came home on the *Independence*. A fine ship, she was then a popular American choice, an alternative, on the US–Mediterranean run. She too docked at Pier 84.

'The *Colombo* had about four cargo holds, two in the front and two in the rear,' added Palermo:

Watching the cargo being loaded and offloaded at Mediterranean ports was a happy pastime for me. There were great nets filled with goods, big wooded crates and often long American automobiles, especially heavy Cadillacs and Lincolns, coming and going. Some first-class passengers travelled with their own cars or, in cabin, their own camper vans.

The *Colombo* was paired with the new, larger *Leonardo da Vinci* beginning in June 1960. Later, upon the arrival of the even larger sister ships *Michelangelo* and *Raffaello*, the *Colombo* was reassigned to the more lengthy Adriatic service, to Trieste and Venice. She replaced the *Saturnia* and *Vulcania*. The routing was very similar with the exception of the addition of a call at Piraeus. She called at Halifax westbound and at Boston on most eastbound sailings.

I was aboard the *Colombo* in September 1969, but for a very short voyage. My journal entry read:

To surprise a friend, who was returning from Italy, another friend and I flew from New York up to Halifax for the ship's two-day run to New York. The fare

was $25. We were placed in a tourist-class cabin that must have been two or three decks below the waterline. Its only advantage was a continuous musical serenade of slamming water and, of course, the sharks were on the other side of the hull. We hit a pea-soup fog off New England and, being the sister ship of the *Andrea Doria*, one couldn't help thinking of that ship's disastrous end. Otherwise, everyone seemed quite pleased with the *Colombo*. She left the impression on us of being a true transatlantic liner that had few frills down in tourist class.

The magnificent *Andrea Doria* arriving in New York for the first time in January 1953. (Italian Line)

Clockwise from left: the superb *Andrea Doria* departing Genoa (Italian Line); The *Cristoforo Colombo* departing Genoa on her maiden crossing to New York in July 1954. (Italian Line); The 700ft-long *Doria* at New York's Pier 84. (ALF Collection)

Sister ships: the *Andrea Doria* and *Cristoforo Colombo* moored together at Genoa. (Italian Line)

First class aboard the *Cristoforo Colombo*. (Italian Line)

Rather abruptly, in early 1973, in a reorganisation of the deficit-ridden Italian Line, the *Colombo* was moved on to the South American service to replace the mechanically troubled *Giulio Cesare*. There were no notices, certainly no fanfare for a farewell sailing and all the *Colombo*'s further North Atlantic sailings were cancelled. She was now teamed at least for a few more years with the *Augustus*. But by the mid 1970s, the Italian Line was in deep financial trouble that was further complicated by much increased oil prices as well as nagging, often disruptive labour problems. Passenger figures had declined considerably and the Italian government was subsidising each passenger carried on the Italian Line with $700. More and more frequently the staff outnumbered the fare-paying guests. In early 1976, in yet further Italian Line reshuffling, the *Augustus* was retired and Lloyd Triestino's *Guglielmo Marconi* was brought over from the equally struggling Italy–Australia trade to assist the *Colombo* with the last of her South American voyages. Both ships were finished within a year.

In April 1977, the 23-year-old *Colombo* was sold for $7 million to the Venezuelan government. Shortly thereafter, she left Genoa for Matanzas in the Orinoco Estuary to take up her new role as a permanently moored workers' accommodation centre. She would service a local steel plant. Then, in 1980, she was sold again, this time to Taiwanese scrappers. Towed across the vast Pacific, she was delivered at Kaohsiung on 30 June 1981. The wreckers' work did not begin, however. Her owners felt they might get even more

A first-class suite aboard the *Cristoforo Colombo* and which was priced from $1,200 for the nine-day crossing from New York to Naples. (Italian Line)

Italian film queen Anna Magnanni departs from New York aboard the *Cristoforo Colombo*. (Italian Line)

3 FABULOUS MEDITERRANEAN FESTIVAL CRUISES

T/v CRISTOFORO COLOMBO
23 DAYS • 8 FASCINATING PORTS
From New York, October 26, 1963

T/v LEONARDO DA VINCI
23 DAYS • 8 ENCHANTING PORTS
From New York, November 6, 1963

T/v LEONARDO DA VINCI
24 DAYS • 9 GLAMOROUS PORTS
From New York, December 24, 1963

Italian Line
THE SUNNY SOUTHERN ROUTE

HALLOWEEN MEDITERRANEAN FESTIVAL CRUISE

It's witches and goblins, gaiety and moon magic . . it's lots of tricks and all treat as you join in the fun of an unforgettable Halloween Party on the high seas . . . just one of the many thrills awaiting you—both at sea and ashore —on this 23-day Mediterranean Festival Cruise!

T/V CRISTOFORO COLOMBO
23 DAYS • 8 FASCINATING PORTS
From New York, October 26, 1963

PORT	ARRIVAL		DEPARTURE	
NEW YORK			Oct. 26	noon
Tenerife	Nov. 1	8:00 am	Nov. 1	8:00 pm
Gibraltar	Nov. 3	8:00 am	Nov. 3	1:00 pm
Palermo	Nov. 5	8:00 am	Nov. 5	10:00 pm
Naples	Nov. 6	8:00 am	Nov. 7	1:00 pm
Genoa	Nov. 8	7:00 am	Nov. 8	Midnight
Cannes	Nov. 9	8:00 am	Nov. 9	7:00 pm
Barcelona	Nov. 10	8:00 am	Nov. 10	Midnight
Palma de Majorca	Nov. 11	7:00 am	Nov. 11	1:00 pm
Gibraltar	Nov. 12	10:00 am	Nov. 12	11:00 am
NEW YORK	Nov. 18	9:00 am		

FULL CRUISE FARES FROM
$470.00 in Cabin Class
$620.00 in First Class

THANKSGIVING MEDITERRANEAN FESTIVAL CRUISE

The tradition of Thanksgiving, so endearing to all of us, takes on a memorable new aspect as you celebrate it with a sumptuous dinner of turkey and all the trimmings aboard the LEONARDO . . . where every day is a holiday as you cruise from port to port! And, in between, the thrill of visiting ashore—on your own or in organized tours—in the romantic Mediterranean ports.

T/V LEONARDO DA VINCI
23 DAYS • 8 ENCHANTING PORTS
From New York, November 6, 1963

PORT	ARRIVAL		DEPARTURE	
NEW YORK			Nov. 6	noon
Tenerife	Nov. 12	8:00 am	Nov. 12	8:00 pm
Gibraltar	Nov. 14	8:00 am	Nov. 14	1:00 pm
Palermo	Nov. 16	8:00 am	Nov. 16	10:00 pm
Naples	Nov. 17	8:00 am	Nov. 18	1:00 pm
Genoa	Nov. 19	7:00 am	Nov. 19	Midnight
Cannes	Nov. 20	8:00 am	Nov. 20	7:00 pm
Barcelona	Nov. 21	8:00 am	Nov. 21	Midnight
Palma de Majorca	Nov. 22	7:00 am	Nov. 22	1:00 pm
Gibraltar	Nov. 23	10:00 am	Nov. 23	11:00 am
NEW YORK	Nov. 29	9:00 am		

FULL CRUISE FARES FROM
$470.00 in Cabin Class
$620.00 in First Class

CHRISTMAS-NEW YEAR MEDITERRANEAN FESTIVAL CRUISE

What a wonderful way to mark the end of the old year and usher in the new . . . Christmas and New Year Eve parties aboard this luxurious ship, with New Year's Day in captivating Lisbon followed by a gay round of festivities and visits to interesting Mediterranean ports.

T/V LEONARDO DA VINCI
24 DAYS • 9 GLAMOROUS PORTS
From New York, December 24, 1963

PORT	ARRIVAL		DEPARTURE	
NEW YORK	—		Dec. 24	4:00 pm
Las Palmas	Dec. 30	8:00 am	Dec. 30	7:00 pm
Lisbon (1964)	Jan. 1	8:00 am	Jan. 1	8:00 pm
Gibraltar	Jan. 2	noon	Jan. 2	5:00 pm
Palermo	Jan. 4	11:00 am	Jan. 4	10:00 pm
Naples	Jan. 5	8:00 am	Jan. 6	1:00 pm
Genoa	Jan. 7	7:00 am	Jan. 8	2:00 am
Cannes	Jan. 8	9:00 am	Jan. 8	8:00 pm
Barcelona	Jan. 9	9:00 am	Jan. 9	Midnight
Palma de Majorca	Jan. 10	8:00 am	Jan. 10	1:00 pm
Gibraltar	Jan. 11	10:00 am	Jan. 11	11:00 am
NEW YORK	Jan. 17	8:00 am		

FULL CRUISE FARES FROM
$474.00 in Cabin Class
$629.00 in First Class

Italian Line itineraries. (Andrew Kilk Collection)

Mediterranean cruising. (Andrew Kilk Collection)

money on the resale market and so moved the *Colombo* to Hong Kong for more convenient inspection by prospective buyers. Unfortunately, there were no takers. In July 1983, she returned to Kaohsiung and was promptly scrapped. Barely noticed, the era of great post-war Italian liners was just about gone completely.

The *Cristoforo Colombo* at Genoa – with the French *Bretagne* just across the shed and the *Giulio Cesare* beyond. (ALF Collection)

Winter's day: *Andrea Doria* at New York. (ALF Collection)

Tragedy: the *Doria* sinking on the morning of 26 July 1956. (ALF Collection)

Final plunge for the *Doria*. (ALF Collection)

4

OTHER ITALIANS, OTHER ROUTES

Adriatica Line: *Ausonia*

Along with the Italian Line, Tirrenia Lines and Lloyd Triestino, another member of the Italian government's Finmare Group was the Venice-based Adriatica Line. TIts interests were in the eastern Mediterranean – from Italy to Greece, Turkey, Lebanon, Israel, Cyprus and Syria. Most of their forty-two-ship pre-Second World War fleet was lost by 1945. Their lone survivor was the 9,314-ton *Esperia*. New builds included the 5,100-ton *Enotria* and *Messapia*; the 4,755-ton *San Giorgio* and *San Marco*; the 4,350-ton *Bernina*, *Brennero* and *Stelvio*; and, largest of all, the 11,879-ton *Ausonia*.

The late Laurence Dunn, the well-known maritime author and marine designer, called the 522ft-long *Ausonia* 'a ship of very advanced design with extremely fine contemporary-style accommodation and furnishing'. Unquestionably, she was one of Italy's finest liners of the post-war era. She followed the splendid design of the *Andrea Doria* and *Cristoforo Colombo* and then lent her own influences to Costa's upcoming *Federico C* of 1958. The

Ausonia entered service in October 1957 and was soon marketed as 'the largest and fastest liner operating solely within the Mediterranean'. Thouh she had 20-knot service speed, she did reach over 23 knots during her sea trials.

Together with the *Esperia*, the 529-passenger *Ausonia* maintained Adriatica's 'Grand Express' run – Trieste, Venice and Brindisi to Alexandria and Beirut.

The *Ausonia* sailed in Adriatica service for exactly twenty years until withdrawn in September 1977. This also marked the end of Adriatica's conventional passenger ship service. Hereafter, the company would run only ferries. Finmare took the *Ausonia* and placed her on charter to the newly established Italian Line Cruises International, which was also operating the *Galileo Galilei* and *Guglielmo Marconi* at the time. Later, in 1982, the *Ausonia* was reassigned to the Grimaldi-Siosa Group.

Finally sold out of Italian service in 1998, the *Ausonia* joined the Greek-owned Louis Cruise Lines and did charter cruising until renamed *Ivory* in 2005. She was retired in 2009 and scrapped in the following year at Alang in India.

Completed in 1949, Adriatica Line's *Esperia* sailing from Venice. (Adriatica Line)

The handsome, 1957-built *Ausonia*'s design was based on the earlier *Andrea Doria*. (Alex Duncan)

Home Lines: *Homeric*

'Home Lines was born soon after the Second World War, in early 1946, and was a combination of the Cosulich Company [the same Italian firm who owned such pre-war liners as the *Saturnia* and *Vulcania*], the Swedish American Line and a Greek shipowner, Eugen Eugenides,' recalled the late Captain Mario Vespa, who worked for the Cosulich Line in the 1920s and '30s, and then, beginning in 1946, served with the Home Lines for forty years. The Home Lines was, in fact an early combination of two largely forgotten passenger firms: the Panamanian Lines, which was managed by Cosulich interests out of Trieste, and the South Atlantic Lines, owned partly by Swedish American.

While the *Argentina*, the former Norwegian *Bergensfjord* of 1913, was the very first passenger ship in the Home Lines fleet, the 18,563-ton *Homeric* was among the most popular. With sale details written on the back of a menu in a San Francisco restaurant, she had been the 1931-built *Mariposa* of the Matson Line. A fine pre-war liner, she was not restored after wartime service as a trooper, laid idle until 1953 and then, after rebuilding, reappeared as the restyled *Homeric* in January 1955.

Refitted to carry 147 first-class and 1,096 tourist-class passengers, the 638ft-long *Homeric* spent part of her year (April through October) on the North Atlantic, sailing between Cuxhaven (Hamburg), Le Havre, Southampton, Québec City and Montréal. In winter, she cruised from New York to the Caribbean, mostly on fourteen-night itineraries, and was soon the 'fun ship'. She was noted for her ambience and her fine Italian staff, service and cooking.

A pioneer of today's huge cruise industry, the *Homeric* was damaged in a fire at sea on 1 July 1973 and, being too old for costly repairs, was sold a year later to Taiwanese scrappers.

The *Homeric* at Cuxhaven in her maiden season on the North Atlantic in 1955. (Author's Collection)

Idle at Genoa, the *Homeric* (left) and the *Caribia 2* (ex-*Sydney*) in 1973. (Antonio Scrimali)

Another fine Home Lines' ship, the *Italia*, which was the *Kungsholm* of 1928. (ALF Collection)

Flotta Lauro: *Achille Lauro* & *Angelina Lauro*

After the Second World War, there was a great exodus of Europeans to North as well as South America and to Australia. The concept of 'new lives' beckoned, bringing with it social, political and economic freedom. The Italians were no exceptions and, departing from war-ravaged Genoa, Naples and other port cities, they boarded ships bound for the likes of New York, Buenos Aires and Sydney. Based in Naples, Flotta Lauro, which had operated cargo ships, saw great opportunity (and profit) in the migrant trades, especially to far-off Australia. By the early 1950s, it began operating two greatly rebuilt passenger ships, the 14,000-ton *Roma* and *Sydney*. They were routed from Genoa, Naples and Messina to Fremantle, Melbourne and Sydney via Port Said, the Suez Canal, Aden and Colombo. They had been US-flag 'baby flattops', small aircraft carriers built on standardised C-3 type freighter hulls that were constructed in the Second World War. Shipowner Achille Lauro, the one-time mayor of Naples, bought them as post-war surplus – at bargain prices – and rebuilt them for 119 passengers in first class and 994 in tourist class. Painted all over in white, they looked quite attractive and certainly seemed more modern than they actually were. Lauro had one other passenger ship, the *Surriento*, a former Grace Line passenger-cargo ship, the *Santa Maria*, but which was used on the Italy–Latin America trade.

'First class on the *Roma* and *Sydney* was quite beautiful,' remembered Tony Ralph, who saw the pair at Sydney in the 1960s:

They had glossy lino floors, modern styles and, although small converted ships, were actually quite elegant. There were two promenade decks – both of which were quite narrow, however. The *Roma* and *Sydney* stood out in their day. Their contemporary Italian decor was, to Australians, quite startling. Australians were used to the very conservative, wooded interiors of the British flag P&O liners.

In the early 1960s, 'Lauro actually thought of building two brand-new liners for the still booming Italy–Australia trade, but decided instead to convert two older liners,' according to Tony Ralph:

They bought two of Holland's finest passenger liners, the *Willem Ruys* [1947] and the *Oranje* [1939]. It was all very exciting, but personally I missed them as Dutch ships. They were very interesting and both had been regular callers at Sydney for years. In preparation, Lauro even opened new offices in the best location in Sydney and had two superb models of the new ships on show in the windows. They arrived, by 1966, as the *Achille Lauro* and *Angelina Lauro*. They were splendid ships, groundbreaking in every way. They had a big impact on the Australian liner trade back then. They were sensations! They were also very elegant, but in a very modern sense. They represented fantastic transformations. The carved woods and the heavy Dutch furniture were replaced by stainless steel, Formica and lino. They were Italian modern throughout. And on the outside, they were topped-off by great winged funnels.

'The pair offered an express service from Genoa and Naples, and occasionally included calls at Beirut as well, and were among the first passenger ships to offer innovative returns to Europe,' he added:

To recruit more European-bound passengers, they sometimes sailed home via Cape Horn and the East Coast of South America, which altogether offered an interesting itinerary and new ports of call for the Australians. They also offered many cruises from Sydney, spaced between the line voyages, to places like Bali, Singapore and the South Pacific islands.

While the original *Roma* and *Sydney* were long since sold and eventually broken up, the 23,000-ton *Achille Lauro* and the 21,000-ton *Angelina Lauro* turned mostly to cruising after 1973, soon after the jumbo jets arrived in full force as fierce competitors to Australia-routed liners. The *Angelina Lauro*,

A former 'baby flattop', a small aircraft carrier, the *Roma* made a fine-looking passenger ship if smaller at only 492ft in length. (ALF Collection)

The *Angelina Lauro* burns at St Thomas in the Caribbean in 1979. (Author's Collection)

run by Costa Line in later years, burned at St Thomas in the Caribbean in March 1979 and afterwards, in September, her burnt-out hull sank in the Pacific while en route to Taiwanese scrappers. The *Achille Lauro*, then operated by other Italians, MSC Cruises, and made internationally famous following a terrorist hijacking in the eastern Mediterranean in October 1985, met a similar fate. She sank off East Africa in December 1994 after being abandoned following a fire at sea. By then, Flotta Lauro had gone as well, having collapsed into bankruptcy in the early 1980s.

Sitmar: *Castel Felice*

Sitmar – an abbreviation for Societa Italiana Trasporti Marittima – was created by Alexander Vlasov (hence the 'V' on all Sitmar funnels), a Russian who fled his native Odessa in 1917. Together with his son Boris, he settled first in Romania, then in Poland and finally in Italy. Vlasov had a keen, highly intuitive aptitude for shipping, beginning with freighters. His company's first passenger ship was the 12,478-ton *Castel Felice*, the former *Kenya* of the British India Line, dating from 1930. She was rebuilt at Genoa in 1951 and afterwards carried migrants to Australia as well as the east coast of South America, the Caribbean and Venezuela. There were even a few appearances on the North Atlantic, putting into New York, Montréal and Québec City. Her passenger quarters were arranged for twenty-eight in first class and 1,173 in tourist class (and finally to 1,405 all-tourist class). Captain Franco Donnino served aboard the 493ft-long *Castel Felice* and recalled, 'She was a

very solid old ship, an excellent "sea boat", and could make the passage from Southampton to Sydney via Suez in thirty-four days.'

Sitmar went on to convert several passenger ships – namely the *Fairsea*, *Fairsky* and *Fairstar* – and later concentrated primarily on the Europe–Australia and around-the-world liner trades. Later trading in the cruise business, the company was bought out by Princess Cruises in 1988 and the Sitmar name disappeared.

Cogedar Line: *Aurelia*

Another Italian shipowner interested in the Europe–Australian migrant trade was the Cogedar Line – abbreviated from Compagnia Genovese di Armamento. At various times they employed three converted passenger ships, each with considerable low-fare, all-tourist-class accommodation. There was the 8,776grt *Flaminia*, a former American freighter dating from 1922 and rebuilt with passenger quarters in 1949; the *Aurelia*, a one-time German combination passenger-cargo ship; and, finest and fanciest of all in the Cogedar fleet, the 15,500grt *Flavia*, formerly Cunard's *Parthia*, a passenger-cargo liner used on the Liverpool–New York run. The long-lived *Aurelia* was also a transatlantic passenger ship at times.

During the 1950s and '60s, a number of simple, quite austere passenger ships sailed the North Atlantic. They were not, say, in the same league as the far larger *Queen Mary* or *Île de France* or the speedy *United States*. On mostly summertime voyages, they carried low-fare passengers: students, their teachers and chaperones, and tour guides. Perhaps the most popular of these so-called 'student ships' were the Dutch-flag sisters *Groote Beer*, *Waterman* and *Zuiderkruis*. Carrying up to 900 all-tourist-class passengers, they were converted wartime-built Victory ships. But there were others, such as the ships of the Swiss-owned Arosa Line, West Germany's *Seven Seas*, Sitmar's *Castel Felice* and Italy's *Aurelia*.

Professor Alex Garcia sailed aboard the 10,840grt *Aurelia* in the 1960s. He was aboard one of her summer runs between New York, Le Havre and Southampton, under charter to the Manhattan-headquartered Council on Student Travel. 'We were full to capacity, about 1,100 in all, on that otherwise smallish ship – but it was all great fun, exciting and enriching,' he remembered:

The *Castel Felice* was very popular on the Europe–Australia run. (ALF Collection)

It was rather slow, a nine-day crossing, and there were lots of lectures and slide shows on art and architecture. There were two choral groups aboard and they gave concerts. There were also concerts of recorded music. Actually, there was more going on than aboard some of today's cruise ships – and it was all more exciting and interesting than bingo and dance class. And the Italian cooking was excellent. The eastbound voyage cost $175 or just under $20 a day. At Southampton, we took the 'boat train' up to London. Coming home, a few months later, I took the very big, very fast *United States*, which was quite a contrast to the dear little *Aurelia*.

The 487ft-long *Aurelia* normally sailed on the Europe–Australia run, from Bremerhaven, Rotterdam and Southampton via the Suez Canal to Fremantle, Melbourne and Sydney. But summers were the 'slack season' on the 'down under' trade and so the summer Atlantic voyages were a profitable alternative.

The 17-knot *Aurelia* was originally built in 1939 at the famed Blohm & Voss shipyard of Hamburg. She was then called *Huascaran*, sailing for the Hamburg America Line between northern Europe and ports along the west coast of South America (Guayaquil, Callao, Valparaíso etc.). She was then a combination passenger-cargo ship, carrying only thirty-two passengers in total. She survived the Second World War, only to be given to the Canadian government as reparations. Renamed *Beaverbrae* and later sold outright to Canadian Pacific Steamships, she sailed between Bremerhaven and Québec City, carrying up to 773 migrants westbound, but then returning only as a cargo vessel.

Cogedar bought the ship in 1954 and refitted her as the *Aurelia*. Afterwards, she could carry 1,124 all-tourist-class passengers in more comfortable, fully air-conditioned quarters. Her Australian sailings ended in 1968 and, after a brief, unsuccessful stint as a cruise ship – which included the collapse of Cogedar and being 'arrested' for debts – she was sold to Greece's Chandris Cruises in 1970 and became their *Romanza*. She cruised the Mediterranean and Red Sea, the Caribbean and around South America. She was the setting, in the late 1980s, for an episode of the British detective series *Rumpole of the Bailey*. Dancing, drama and detectives!

Chandris sold the ship in 1991 to Cypriot buyers Ambassador Leisure Cruises, who renamed her *Romantica* for use on three- and four-day air-sea cruises between Cyprus, Israel and Egypt. But these owners went bankrupt in 1995 and the ex-*Aurelia* was laid up. She was later resurrected by another Cypriot company, New Paradise Cruises, and ran the same short cruise schedule in the eastern Mediterranean.

Her days were numbered, however. On 4 October 1997, the then 58-year-old ship burned out during a cruise with 700 passengers and crew aboard. The blaze began in the engine room. The disaster further brought to light the ills of very elderly passenger ships. Ironically, the principal rescue ship was an even older vessel, the 62-year-old *Princesa Victoria*, the one-time *Dunnottar Castle* and later the cruise ship *Victoria*.

Grimaldi-Siosa Lines: *Irpinia*

Grimaldi-Siosa Lines was another Italian firm that cashed in on the booming post-war migrant trade. Its interests were mainly from Europe to Latin America. They also profited from the westward trade of migrants from the Caribbean to England. Similarly to other, mostly Italian-flag, lines it used second-hand ships, often with expanded capacities, on sometimes varied, sometimes short-lived services. In the late 1950s, Grimaldi-Siosa ran a summer season transatlantic schedule – from the Mediterranean to eastern Canada. It also ran periodic voyages to New York.

'The Grimaldi brothers were nephews of Achille Lauro, the founder and owner of Flotta Lauro, the Lauro Line,' noted Ugo Frangini, a purser for thirty years with Grimaldi-Siosa. 'Their mother, Amelia Grimaldi, was the sister of Achille Lauro. But while Lauro was based in Naples, the Grimaldis worked mostly out of Genoa.'

Operating alongside ships such as the *Auriga*, *Centauro* and *Ascania*, and later the larger *Venezuela* (the former French *De Grasse* and later Canadian Pacific's *Empress of Australia*), the 13,204-grt *Irpinia* was the Siosa flagship for some years. Originally built in 1929, by the famed Swan, Hunter & Wigham Richardson shipyard at Newcastle, she was first owned by a long-gone, Marseilles-based firm called Transport Maritimes. She was named *Campana* and sailed out of Marseilles to the east coast of South America – to Rio de Janeiro, Santos, Montevideo and Buenos Aires.

After the fall of France in June 1940, she was laid up at Buenos Aires and later seized outright by the Argentinians. For a time she was called *Rio Jachal*, and made voyages that included occasional trips to the United States. But in 1946, with the war over, she was returned to the French and again sailed to South America as well as to French colonial Indochina. She was sold to Grimaldi-Siosa in 1955. She was rebuilt at a Genovese shipyard, being given a new raked bow in the process. Her original three-class quarters were rearranged to take 187 in first class and 1,034 in tourist class.

Initially, the 537ft-long *Irpinia* sailed between the Mediterranean and the West Indies, often carrying migrants to new lives in Venezuela. In 1959–60 she made summertime Atlantic crossings between Palermo, Naples, Genoa,

Gibraltar, Azores, Québec City and Montréal. 'We carried mostly Hungarian migrants to Canada,' remembered Ugo Frangini, the ship's one-time chief purser. 'The *Irpinia* was actually chartered to a relief organisation that brought these migrants through Austria to the ports of Genoa and Naples.'

In 1962, the 15-knot liner had another facelift. This time, her original twin funnels were replaced by a single, tapered stack; new Fiat diesels replaced her original steam turbines and her passenger quarters were again modernised. Hereafter, she sailed from England, Spain and Portugal to the Caribbean – carrying Spanish and Portuguese migrants on her outbound trip and returning with West Indian, mostly Jamaican, migrants heading for England. The full itinerary varied, but generally read outwards from Southampton: Corunna, Vigo, Madeira, Barbados, Trinidad, La Guaira, Curaçao, Kingston, Ciudad de Trujillo, St Kitts, Montserrat, Antigua, Madeira, Lisbon, Vigo and return to Southampton. By 1970, however, the *Irpinia* turned mostly to cruising – usually on week-long runs out of Genoa around the western Mediterranean, calling at Cannes, Barcelona, Palma, Tunis, Palermo and Capri. Then her seven-day voyages were priced from $79; a two-week Christmas–New Year cruise to the Canaries from $134.

In 1976, just as the 47-year-old ship was about to be retired, she was chartered to an American film company for a starring role in *Voyage of the Damned*. Two temporary 'dummy' funnels were put aboard for her portrayal (mostly while berthed at Barcelona) of the Nazi-German liner *St Louis* making its historic 1939 voyage from Germany to Havana with 900 Jewish refugees on board. 'We spent lots of time at dock, but also went out to sea on occasion to film the sea sequences,' recalled Ugo Frangini. 'The ship was loaded with all sorts of film equipment, a kind of floating Hollywood studio. The director even used Siosa sailors as extras.'

After the filming was completed, her owner, by then retitled simply as Siosa Lines, obviously had some second thoughts about her future. She resumed Mediterranean cruising for several more years, until 1981, by which time she was 52. 'She was finally retired because she could no longer get an Italian classification for seaworthiness,' added Frangini. Laid up for two years at La Spezia, near Genoa, she finally met with the wreckers. Her long career was over, but several years afterwards some furniture and other fittings appeared in second-hand shops in and around La Spezia. These were the last links to Italy's *Irpinia*.

5

PORTUGAL AND SPAIN

Companhia Colonial: *Santa Maria*

After the Second World War, Portugal added several new liners for migrant services to Latin America as well as to the busy colonial links to Africa. There were the 13,100-ton sisters *Imperio* and *Patria*, completed in 1947–48, for Companhia Colonial. Then there was a similar pair, the 13,000-ton *Angola* and *Moçambique,* for Companhia Nacional. The two most prominent Portuguese liners, however, were the handsome-looking sisters *Santa Maria* and *Vera Cruz*.

The 609ft-long liner *Santa Maria* was rather unique in the annals of post-Second World War transatlantic shipping. She was the only Portuguese liner to make regular crossings to North America. She actually ran a rather unusual service, from Europe across the mid-Atlantic to the Caribbean and then up to Florida. And she was, in the 1950s, the only Atlantic passenger ship to use what was then the infant port of Port Everglades, a developing harbour that was the gateway to Florida's Fort Lauderdale and then to Miami, some 17 miles south.

The 20,906grt *Santa Maria* was a particularly striking-looking ship: dove-grey hull, soft yellow upperworks, a single, striped funnel, a mast above the wheelhouse and sets of freight-handling kingposts and booms fore and aft. She was built in 1953 by the Belgians, at the Cockerill-Ougrée shipyard at Hoboken, near Antwerp. She and her sister were actually designed for the Portuguese–South America service, particularly for Portugal's link with Brazil, sailing between Lisbon, Funchal on the island of Madeira and then across to Recife, Salvador, Rio de Janeiro and turnaround at Santos. Appropriately for that service, the accommodation aboard these 20-knot sisters was divided into three classes. The *Santa Maria*, for example, carried 156 in luxurious, upper-deck first class, 226 in less luxurious cabin class and 696 in third class, in large cabins as well as dormitories.

But this South American trade gradually fell away for the ships' owners, the Lisbon-based Companhia Colonial de Navegaçao, so that both ships

At the shipyard: the very handsome, 21,765grt *Vera Cruz*. (ALF Collection)

were eventually reassigned – the 609ft-long *Santa Maria* took her place on a more northern Atlantic service, sailing from Lisbon and Vigo to Funchal, Tenerife, La Guaira (for Caracas), Curaçao, Havana (changed to San Juan after the Castro regime came to power in 1959) and finally to Port Everglades. Meanwhile, the *Vera Cruz* turned to African sailings out to Portuguese-held Angola and Mozambique, mostly carrying troops and government-sponsored passengers.

A modernised, sleek version of the *Santa Maria* and *Vera Cruz*, the *Infante Dom Henrique* was commissioned in 1961. (Companhia Colonial)

Ocean liner enthusiast and traveller Lawton Thomas is rather unique in having made a crossing on the *Santa Maria*; the ship seems not to have been a popular choice amongst regular Atlantic passengers. The year was 1964. 'I had gone over to Europe, to the Mediterranean, from New York on the *Queen Frederica*,' he recalled:

I thought the *Santa Maria*, sailing from Lisbon to Port Everglades, was a different type of trip for a return. Third class was completely full with migrants, all of them bound for La Guaira in Venezuela. I was in cabin class, which was beautifully maintained and which offered superb food and service. First class had a luncheon buffet by their pool, but cabin class did not. The first class section was actually quite small and had an interchangeable area between first and cabin.

On the last half of the trip, from La Guaira through the Caribbean to Port Everglades, Thomas was upgraded to a first-class stateroom. What a treat!

'While the wines were free in cabin class, you actually had to pay for them in first class since they came from the ship's elaborate wine cellar,' he noted:

The decor was very 1950s – nothing really grand, but all 'woody' and 'clubby'. The cabins were large and paneled. Expectedly, there was very little in the way of entertainment. In fact, the ship was actually quite empty after La Guaira. Many of the other first-class passengers were making a full thirty-day cruise, Lisbon–Lisbon. I also had my car in the hold, the cost of transporting it being almost as much as a passenger fare. Actually, I was very thrilled to be making that trip. I had tried to sail in the *Santa Maria* earlier, back in 1958, but then she was fully booked for months ahead.

The *Santa Maria* had become world famous. She made international headlines when, long before the *Achille Lauro* incident of 1985, the ship was hijacked by Portuguese political terrorists while at sea and for some days lost radio contact with an otherwise anxious outside world. The rebels had joined the ship at Curaçao on 22 January 1961 and then seized control days later while she was sailing off Martinique. The third officer was shot and several other crew members injured in the takeover, which was a protest against the politics of Portuguese dictator António Salazar. They planned to sail the ship and her passengers to Angola. But after radio communications were restored the hijackers agreed to land the 600 or so passengers in Brazil. The ship reached Recife on 2 February, landed the worried guests and was about to sail to Africa, but warships stood at the harbour entrance. The ship's fate was sealed; the crew refused to cooperate, and the terrorists finally surrendered.

By the early 1970s, like most other Atlantic liners the *Santa Maria* was facing a declining trade, financial losses and the general infirmities of a passenger ship turning 20 years of age. But it was the dramatic and sudden increase in fuel prices that finally convinced her owners to withdraw the ship. The market was so low for second-hand liners in 1973–74 that only Far Eastern scrap merchants offered low but acceptable bids. And so, in the spring of 1973, the *Santa Maria*, manned by a small crew and carrying no passengers, sailed off for Kaohsiung on Taiwan, where she was later broken up.

Compañía Trasatlántica: *Covadonga & Guadalupe*

Intended to be freighters, twin sisters *Covadonga* and *Guadalupe* were in a way the primary units of Compañía Trasatlántica, also known as the Spanish Line. Built in 1953, these 10,226-tonners carried 105 in first class and some 245 in tourist class. Enduring until the early 1970s (but in later years as twelve-berth freighters), they worked a triangular route: Bilbao, Santander, Gijón, Vigo, Lisbon, Cádiz, New York, Havana (changed to San Juan after 1959), Veracruz and then in reverse.

Ybarra Line: *Cabo San Roque & Cabo San Vicente*

Two very handsome liners of the late 1950s were the 14,500-ton sisters *Cabo San Roque* and *Cabo San Vicente*. They were originally designed as twin stackers, but instead were given contemporary profiles and fitted with modern-style quarters for 189 cabin-class and 652 tourist-class passengers. Owned by Seville-based Ybarra & Company, the ships were used on the busy Europe–South America run, from Genoa via Marseilles, Barcelona, Cádiz, Lisbon and Tenerife then across to Bahia, Rio de Janeiro, Santos, Montevideo and Buenos Aires. Both the 556ft-long liners also offered periodic cruises.

6

GREECE

National Hellenic American Line: *Queen Frederica*

The 21,500-ton *Queen Frederica* was popular, one of the great beloved Greek liners on the Atlantic. She sailed between Piraeus, other Mediterranean ports and New York, in direct competition with Greek Line's *Olympia*. Westbound migrants in tourist class were a large part of their trade, but there were also first-class travellers. Charlotte Green was aboard the 582ft-long *Frederica* in September 1964:

> We traveling from New York to Piraeus and the trip included a special stop at Barcelona. The entire first-class section was filled with Spanish royalty and other aristocrats going to Athens for the royal wedding of Princess Sophia of Greece and Prince Juan Carlos, the future king of Spain. Servants, chauffeurs, even personal hairdressers were put in tourist class simply because there were not enough first-class staterooms available. One American couple in a first-class suite was given financial compensation to vacate their quarters, stay in a fine Barcelona hotel and await one of the Italian Line ships that was passing through in a few days.

The *Queen Frederica* was one of the great, well built and very spacious American liners preferred by the Greeks and other Mediterranean ship owners. Strong and sturdy and built of the finest materials, they were ideal for conversion; with greatly increased capacities they still had long careers ahead of them. The *Frederica* had been designed by the brilliant William Francis Gibbs for Matson Line's California–Hawaii service. She was commissioned in 1927 as the *Malolo,* the first major luxury liner in Hawaiian service, and her subsequent success led to a trio of even larger, grander ships: the *Lurline* (later the Greek *Ellinis*), the *Mariposa* (later Home Lines' *Homeric*) and finally the *Monterey* (which became the Chandris *Britanis*). The four were among the most successful, long-lasting liners ever built. In 1937 the *Malolo* was refitted and modernised, and in the process was renamed *Matsonia*. 'She had been too stiff when built and rolled badly,' said Arthur Crook. 'When she was refitted

in 1937–38, the added weight made her a better sea boat. I believe that in her early days she was known as the "Rolling *Malolo*".'

She served during the Second World War as a trooper and then reopened the Hawaiian service, but only in a partially restored state. In 1948, she was cleared for sale by the US government to foreign interests, being sold to the multinational Home Lines, raising the Panamanian flag and being renamed *Atlantic.* She did Atlantic service, both from the Mediterranean and from northern ports, before being transferred in December 1954 to a new Home Lines' subsidiary, the National Hellenic American Line, for Greek-flag service to New York. She was to be the rival to Greek Line's new *Olympia,* which, to the unhappiness of the Greek government, was under the Liberian flag.

'Mr Eugenides, one of the founders of the Home Lines, was a great friend to Queen Frederika, the wife of King Paul of Greece,' noted Captain Mario Vespa, a vice president and long-time employee of the Home Lines:

> The royal family was upset as well about the *Olympia* being under the Liberian colours. National Hellenic American was created with the queen's blessing. It was all a great success, possibly much to the annoyance of the Goulandris people who ran the *Olympia*. The *Queen Frederica* was a huge success, one of the greatest of all for the Home Lines in those days.

By the early 1960s, however, Home Lines accepted airline domination on the Atlantic and wanted out of transoceanic service. Instead, it was interested only in cruising, which it intuitively felt had an enormous future. Even the big *Oceanic,* building for the Hamburg–Montréal run, was soon reassigned to year-round cruising, weekly seven-day voyages between New York and Nassau. The *Queen Frederica* endured until 1965, when she was sold to Chandris Lines, who believed there was still some future, if only very seasonally, on the Mediterranean–New York run. Additionally, Chandris wanted a greater entrée with the US travel market, which included future cruise services. The veteran *Frederica* was the ticket. When I travelled in her for a late summer cruise to Bermuda in September 1967, she was actually

The *Queen Frederica* departs from Genoa. (ALF Collection)

past her best. Old piping was leaking, the teak decking needed work and the steam whistles struggled. New safety regulations enacted by the US Coast Guard soon kept her away from American ports and she was reassigned to Southampton–Australia–New Zealand migrant sailings. Still very profitable, she was often booked to every last upper bunk. 'She was a fabulous old lady of the sea. I have pleasant memories, but I am sure that she wasn't really seaworthy any longer,' remembered Gregory Maxwell:

> I emigrated from Australia to Britain aboard her in 1966. It was $130, which included a train ticket from the Southampton Docks up to London. We sailed from Fremantle by way of Colombo, Aden, Port Said and Piraeus. The ship was filled with young Australians traveling the world, returning Greeks who disliked Australia and other Greeks who were going home to bring more Greeks out to Melbourne and Sydney. In those days, these migrants were called the 'New Australians'. There was still a big need for manual-labour people in Australia in the 1960s.

The ship was nearly lost when, during a positioning trip without passengers from Villefranche to Piraeus on 4 November 1969, there was a fire. At the time she was some 70 miles south of Piraeus. Repairs were made when the ship was laid up for the winter.

But even in deepening old age, she had her loyal followers. Captain Dimitrios Chilas spent fifteen years with Chandris Lines, some of them on the then 45-year-old *Queen Frederica*:

> She was in many ways the Company's grandest ship. She had Corinthian columns in the lounge, a balcony for an orchestra in the dining room and the general feel of a 'real ship'. We were running seven-day cruises out of Genoa to western Mediterranean ports under charter to Sun Cruises in the early 1970s.

Laid up after the 1973 summer season in the Mediterranean, the *Frederica* spent her final years in that great Greek graveyard of older ships: Perama Bay. It was a sort of 'maritime retirement home'. While there were rumours that she might become a hotel ship in Egypt and later that a film company wanted to use her as a floating prop in scenes for *Raise the Titanic*, she was in fact passed over to local Greek scrappers in 1977. In the midst of demolition, fires were started to burn the old teak off her outer decks. One of the most interesting liners of the twentieth century was soon finished off.

Greek Line: *Olympia*

'The stories of her actually being an aircraft carrier for the Royal Navy are untrue. She was designed and created as a liner from the start,' said James Wheeler, a naval architect for the Goulandris family, the owners of the Greek Line:

> The *Olympia* was the pride of the fleet from the start. She was the first large liner built for the Greeks and a ship well ahead of her time. I remember that when she was completed, the British public called her 'garish'. They said that she was too modern, even for 1953.

Wheeler had worked for Cammell Laird, the well-known British shipbuilders, from 1947–56 and then joined a company called Maritime Technical Administration, which was owned by the technical manager of the Greek Line. He never actually worked directly with the Greek Line, but very closely to them.
  The Greek Line had their *Nea Hellas* on the Piraeus–New York run along with several other mainly small and rather elderly ships, such as the *Neptunia*, *Columbia* and *Canberra*, on other Atlantic services. But they wanted something different, something much better. The Second World War was long over and European travel was steadily increasing along with a renewed burst of westbound migration headed for North American shores. The Greek government was supportive as well, wanting a large liner to fly the national colours as a representative. In the Mediterranean, the American Export Lines had just added its 29,500-ton sisters *Independence* and *Constitution* and the Italian Line was building the 29,000-ton *Andrea Doria* and *Cristoforo Colombo*. Even the Israelis were coming out with new tonnage, smaller but competitive, such as the 9,900-ton sister ships *Israel* and *Zion*. Greece could not be left out. The Greek Line turned to a yard up in Scotland, Alexander Stephen & Sons, based near Glasgow. A single 23,000-tonner was planned.
  'Basil Goulandris, the owner of the Greek Line, helped design her, but died before completion. His son John Goulandris took over and followed with the ship's design,' according to Wheeler:

It was unusual for a ship of that size to have so many public rooms. They were actually spread about. There was actually no full deck of public rooms. The main lounge was called the Zebra Room, but this was later considered a great mistake. The decor, with all those black stripes, was not helpful in rough seas. The ship was well designed as a two-class liner. The first and tourist class sections were very definite with complete separation. The 130 or so passengers in first class almost never knew that there were 1,200 or so in tourist class. The *Olympia* also had some good open-deck arrangements, which were again segregated because of the two classes. They ship also offered some great menus for the 1950s.

'The *Olympia* was pleasant in many ways and certainly a very good-looking ship, but did have some problems,' added Wheeler:

> Being built without stabilisers was a big mistake. Not everyone believed in fin stabilizers in the 1950s. It was well known, for example, that the fin stabilisers on P&O's *Chusan* later fell off. The *Olympia* was not the greatest 'sea boat'. It was said that she had more storm ropes than any other ship on the Atlantic. Over the years, she encountered some nasty storms. The bridge windows had been smashed and there was lots of flooding.

The original link to Greece was to have been a close one. The 611ft-long ship was intended as the flagship of the entire Greek merchant marine and was to have been named *Frederica*, honouring Queen Frederica, the wife of King Paul. But prior to completion, there were problems with the government over regulation and taxes. The Goulandris family became impatient and eventually lost interest. The ship was finished with Liberian registry and was named *Olympia*. 'It was embarrassing,' noted a Chandris Lines captain years later, 'that the largest Greek liner flew the Liberian flag.' Even in her earliest years, she was kept from Greek waters, being assigned to the North Atlantic rather than Mediterranean service. Because the Germans still had not returned to Atlantic liner service, the Greeks saw greater potential, especially with the migrant trade to North America, and so the 23-knot *Olympia* was assigned to sail in and out of Bremerhaven, with stops at Southampton and Cherbourg, en route to Halifax and New York. Her actual maiden voyage, in October 1953, was a port-filled affair. The route: Glasgow to New York via Belfast, Liverpool, Southampton, Cherbourg, Cobh and Halifax.
  'The *Olympia* started her life with a private cruise over to Dublin from Glasgow with the Goulandris family and their friends aboard,' noted Wheeler:

Another strikingly handsome 1950s liner, the *Olympia*, seen off Dover. (Greek Line)

Later, she was the first passenger ship to go into the King George V Graving Dock at Southampton with a full load of passengers aboard. She needed some mechanical adjustments. Years later, in 1961, she had other, quite unique repairs. Her main gear wheel was changed at Pier 88 in New York using local shipyard assistance.

In 1955, the *Olympia* was moved to the Mediterranean, sailing between Piraeus and New York. Goulandris felt that they needed to compete following the opening of Home Lines' National Hellenic American Line service in December 1954. They were using a good-sized ship, the 21,500-ton *Atlantic*, which had been specially renamed *Queen Frederica*. Home Lines was after all a company with very strong Greek links through the Eugenides family. The *Olympia* and the *Queen Frederica* were fierce competitors, and all the while it was known that the American Export Lines wanted to expand its liner services to Greece as well as to Israel.

The *Olympia* ran occasional winter cruises from New York, usually two-week trips to the sunny isles of the Caribbean, but also an annual eight-week Grand Mediterranean & Black Sea Cruise, limited to a club-like 600 guests and which included the novelty of visiting such Black Sea ports as Odessa, Yalta, Sochi and Varna. The fifty-five-day trip in the early 1960s was priced from $1,300.

Cruise travel specialist John Ferguson recalled of the *Olympia*: 'The food was always good and the all-Greek crew was very pleasant, very friendly. The *Olympia* always had an air of excitement about her, especially at sailing time. It was what you expected of a true luxury liner.'

'The *Olympia* later offered the first regular cruises "to nowhere" out of New York,' added James Wheeler. These began in 1968 and were usually scheduled for a Friday evening departure, two full days at sea and an early return on Monday morning.

The *Olympia* also made numerous seven-day cruises to Bermuda. She carried 3,500 passengers on these cruises in a three-month period in 1968 and nearly 5,000 the following year in a similar period. By October 1968, it was announced that the *Olympia* single-handedly generated nearly $25 million to the economy of Bermuda. By 1970, the ship was actually doing more cruises than transatlantic crossings.

In early 1970 the *Olympia* had was refitted for year-round cruising. Her aft decks were remodelled, the aft mast removed and the berthing rearranged for 1,037 all-one-class passengers. 'The new decor was less than attractive,' noted John Ferguson. 'It was all low budget. There were brown shag rugs and orange or gold velvet bedspreads. It resembled a cheap hotel.'

Financial troubles were starting for the Greek Line as the cruise business became more competitive and as operational costs increased. Even the *Olympia*, once the pride of the company, grew shabby. 'For her Bermuda cruises, the local government complained that the ship looked tacky, poorly maintained,' added Ferguson. 'The Greek Line reacted by painting one side of the ship, the side that faced Hamilton's Front Street!'

It was the oil crisis of 1973–74 that spelled her end under her original owners. About to start a new series of weekly Greek islands cruises from Piraeus, she had too few bookings, her operational costs soared and, as result, she was abruptly laid up. A year later, both she and her last fleet mate, the *Queen Anna Maria*, were bankrupt and 'under arrest'. The 21-knot *Olympia* was laid up for eight long years, rusting, untouched and lonely. Her original stack would eventually crumble from decay. There was talk that she would become a moored hotel ship for the Sheraton Corporation, but then Commodore Cruise Lines of Miami bought her. Rejuvenated at a Hamburg shipyard (which included the removal of her once distinctive funnel), she was back in service, but as the *Caribe I*, in the late summer of 1983.

In May 1993, the *Caribe I* returned to New York, on one- to seven-day cruises, but this time as the *Regal Empress*. At first under charter from Commodore, she was later bought outright by Regal Cruises, a partnership of two local travel firms, Liberty Travel and Gogo Tours. Along with cruises from other US East Coast ports, she often spent her winters cruising from Port Manatee, near Tampa on Florida's west coast. Reports that she was sold to Sea Escape Cruises in October 1993 for 'day cruises' out of Port Everglades, Florida proved false. She was sold in 2003, however, to Imperial Majesty Cruise Lines and began running two-day cruises between Port Everglades and Nassau.

Her long career ended in 2009 when, after being laid up, she was sold to Indian shipbreakers.

Chandris Lines: *Patris*

The first major passenger ship in the Chandris Lines' fleet was the 18,400-ton *Patris*. Built at Harland & Wolff's yard at Belfast in 1950 as Union-Castle Line's *Bloemfontein Castle*, the 595ft-long ship joined the Greeks nine years later. Her capacity was greatly increased from 721 all cabin-class passengers to 1,036 (thirty-six in first class, 1,000 in tourist) and later up to 1,400 for her Chandris owners. A popular as well as very profitable ship, she was suited to her trade: unpretentious passenger quarters blended with a four-hold freight capacity. As the *Patris*, she carried migrants from Europe out to Australia and then on the homeward trips carried Australian budget tourists ('the backpacker set' as one staff member called it) as well as some disgruntled migrants, who were unhappy with Australia. She also returned with large quantities of Australian beef in her freezer compartments, which were left over from her Union-Castle days.

Generally, the 18½-knot *Patris* sailed from Piraeus and Limassol to Fremantle, Melbourne and Sydney via Port Said and Aden. First under the advertising name of the Europe–Australia Line, the Chandris 'down under' service was a huge success. Soon, a string of even larger second-hand liners was added, including the *Ellinis*, the *Australis*, the *Queen Frederica* and the *Britanis*. These other ships did, however, expand the service to northern Europe, to Bremerhaven, Rotterdam and Southampton. They were 'full-up' on every outbound sailing, especially after Anthony Chandris secured the prized Australian government contract to carry the low-fare so-called 'new settlers'. Gregory Maxwell, an Australian who had moved to England in the late 1960s, decided to return home for a visit in 1972. He sailed aboard the *Patris*:

By then, following the closure of the Suez Canal, the *Patris* was sailing out of Djibouti in French Somalia on the East African coast. Chandris flew you down to Djibouti on charter flights … The ship was absolutely full – Yugoslavians,

Formerly the *Lurline*, Chandris Lines' *Ellinis* was a very popular liner on the Australian migrant and tourist run. (ALF Collection)

Italians, Greeks, Turks, even Arabs. I was the only Anglo-Saxon among the passengers. Djibouti, as I remember, was like Fort de France on Martinique – shops, souvenir stands, a tropical outpost of French imports. We sailed with nearly 1,000 passengers and then picked-up 400 French-speaking passengers at Mauritius. Otherwise, I think that the breakdown was something like 300 Greeks, 200 Italians, 200 Yugoslavians and about 300 Arabs and Turks. What a complement! There were five different typewriters for the five different languages to make daily programmes. The Turkish and Arab migrants were from villages in the mountains or from the desert. They were very primitive, almost barbaric. Every one else seemed to stay clear of them. I ate in a separate dining room with the Italians. There were three sittings for dinner: 4, 6 and 7:30.

Soon, however, with rising fuel prices and increased competition from jets that were now regularly flying east of Suez, Chandris had to make further changes. With the likes of the *Ellinis* and the *Britanis* being shifted to almost full-time cruising, the *Patris*, along with the *Australis*, continued on the long, but declining Australian run. While the larger ship remained in European service, the *Patris* was soon placed on a far shorter route, from Singapore to Fremantle, Melbourne and Sydney. Now, her passengers were flown out on cheap charter flights to Singapore and then made the final ten days or so by sea.

Clockwise from left: the veteran *Queen Frederica* was acquired by Chandris in 1965 (ALF Collection); there were countless smaller Greek passenger ships such as the 2,700grt *Lydia* of Hellenic Mediterranean Lines (Alex Duncan); the *Queen Frederica* with the *Oriana* just behind. (ALP Collection)

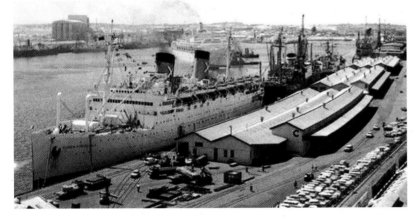

Other passenger ships, the smaller passenger ships of the Greek fleet that traded in the Aegean, the eastern Mediterranean and in the cruise business are far too numerous to mention herein. Most of their ships were rebuilt and some had long, very diverse careers, that included frequent name changes. Such company names that come to mind include Hellenic Mediterranean Lines, Olympic Cruises, Typaldos Lines, Epirotiki Lines, Sun Line, Nomikos Lines and Efthymiadis Lines. None are still trading with the exception of the current Louis Cruise Lines.

A converted Swedish tanker, the *Sophia* belonged to the Greek-flag Efthymiadis Lines. (Michael Cassar)

The *Acropolis* of Typaldos Lines, built in 1932, was the former American liner *Santa Paula*. (Antonio Scrimali)

M/t ATHINAI
(air-conditioned)
and sistership
M/t ACROPOLIS
(air-conditioned)

Length overall 508 ft.
Breadth 72 ft.
Draught 30 ft.
Speed 22 knots
Displacement
17,000 tons

A deck plan for the Typaldos sisters *Athinai* and *Acropolis*. (Andrew Kilk Collection)

7

ISRAEL

Zim Lines: *Israel* & *Zion*

The Haifa-based Zim Lines started passenger operations in the late 1940s with mostly smaller, second-hand tonnage. The company jumped forwards in 1953 with the 11,000-ton *Argentina* of the Home Lines – which in fact dated back to 1913 when she was first commissioned as the Norwegian *Bergensfjord*. Through a West German reparations account, however, new tonnage arrived by the mid 1950s – the 9,800-ton combo liners *Israel* and *Zion* for Haifa–Mediterranean–New York service and the 9,900-ton sisters *Jerusalem* and *Theodor Herzl* for inter-Mediterranean service, mostly between Marseilles, Genoa, Naples and Haifa. While Zim built the far larger 25,500grt *Shalom* in 1964, airline competition as well as expensive Israeli labour spelled a quick end. By the late 1960s, Zim was all but out of the passenger ship business.

A smart-looking passenger-cargo liner, the 9,800-ton *Israel* makes a rare call at Venice in 1955. (Zim Lines)

Israel's *Theodor Herzl* calls at Valletta on Malta during a cruise – with the Bulgarian *Varna* on the left. (ALF Collection)

Night time: the 560-passenger *Theodor Herzl* at Haifa. (Zim Lines)

A rare colour view of the splendid *Rex*, seen along the south side of New York's Pier 92 in 1940. (ALF Collection)

Farewell to Boston: the *Conte Biancamano* makes her final call at the Massachusetts port in 1960. (Author's Collection)

Berthed at Genoa: the *Conte Biancamano* with the *Augustus* behind. (ALF Collection)

The rebuilt, post-war *Conte Grande* seen at Pier 84, New York, in a view dated September 1956. (Author's Collection)

Three Mediterranean passenger ships at Naples: the *Israel* (left), *Independence* and *Augustus*. (Author's Collection)

The *Giulio Cesare* arrives at Genoa with the *Enotria*, *Iskenderun* and *Eugenio C* at dock. (ALF Collection)

Mid-ocean passing: the *Augustus* as seen from the *Giulio Cesare*. (ALF Collection)

The *Augustus* berthed behind the *Oriana*. (ALF Collection)

The handsome *Augustus* departing from New York in 1957. (ALF Collection)

Post-war sensation: the superb-looking *Andrea Doria*. (Italian Line)

The *Cristoforo Colombo* was repainted with a white hull after 1965. (ALF Collection)

Adriatic service: the *Cristoforo Colombo* at Trieste. (ALF Collection)

The gloriously rebuilt *Achille Lauro*, the former Dutch Willem Ruys. (ALF Collection)

In her Italian Lines Cruises International period, the handsome *Ausonia* is seen at Barcelona in a photograph dated 1989. (ALF Collection)

The former *Oranje* as the *Angelina Lauro*, seen at Cape Town. (ALF Collection)

The 1,460-passenger *Fairsky* of Sitmar seen in the South Pacific during a cruise from Sydney. (Tim Noble Collection)

Cogedar Line to Australia: the 10,400grt *Aurelia* at Southampton. (ALF Collection)

Queen of the Portuguese-African liners, the *Infante Dom Henrique*, berthed at Madeira during a cruise. (ALF Collection)

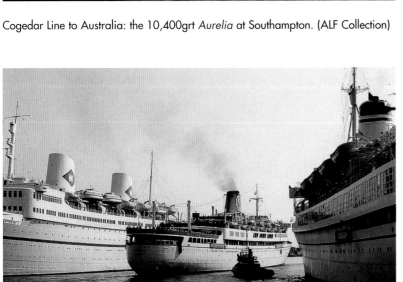

Cruising in the Med: the Greek *Navarino* (left), and then Italy's *Irpinia* (centre) and *Ausonia* (right). (ALF Collection)

One of Spain's largest liners for a time, the 14,900-ton *Cabo San Roque* was designed as a two-class passenger ship for the South American run. (ALF Collection)

The striking *Olympia*, flagship of the Greek Line, seen at New York's Pier 88. (Author's Collection)

The former American liner *Lurline* later became the *Ellinis* for Chandris Lines' Europe–Australia services. (Author's Collection)

The former Dutch *Johan van Oldenbarnevelt* sailed in the early 1960s as the Greek Line's *Lakonia*. (ALF Collection)

The 638ft-long *Ellinis* at Lisbon. (Luis Miguel Correia)

The veteran *Queen Frederica* in Chandris colours departing from Boston. (ALF Collection)

Another long-lived Chandris liner, the *Britanis*, seen at Nassau. (Author's Collection)

Pride of the 1960s Chandris liner fleet, the 33,500grt *Australis* seen berthed at Circular Quay, Sydney. (ALF Collection)

The *Australis* in her final Chandris liner days. (ALF Collection)

The *Britanis* at Cape Town. (ALF Collection)

The former *Pasteur* and later *Bremen*, the *Regina Magna* of Chandris is seen here berthed at San Juan during a winter Caribbean cruise. (Author's Collection)

The former French *Lyautey*. The same ship sailed in later years as the *Lindos* for the Greek-flag Efthymiadis Lines. (Author's Collection)

The ex-Holland America *Ryndam* later sailed as the Epirotiki Lines' *Atlas*. (Author's Collection)

Efthymiadis was rather unique in passenger ship annals because they converted tankers into passenger ships. (Author's Collection)

Clockwise from above: the magnificent *Leonardo da Vinci* at Genoa
(ALF Collection); maiden arrival for the *Leonardo da Vinci* at New
York in July 1960 (Italian Line); the 33,500-ton *Leonardo da Vinci*
at Pier 84, New York. (ALF Collection)

Painted in all
white after
1965, the
*Leonardo da
Vinci* is seen
in this view
at Naples.
(Italian Line)

During a Pacific
cruise from New
York, the *Leonardo
da Vinci* passes
through the Panama
Canal. (Italian Line)

Lloyd Triestino's
Africa berthed at
Genoa. (Author's
Collection)

The former *Victoria* seen in later years as the 'missionary ship' *Anastasis*. (ALF Collection)

The *Donizetti* – the former *Australia* – sailed in Italian Line's west coast of South America service in her latter years. (Author's Collection)

'60s sleek: the good-looking *Guglielmo Marconi* berthed at Melbourne. (Tim Noble Collection)

At Genoa: the *Constitution*, the Soviet *Estonia*, the *Guglielmo Marconi* and (far right) the *Messapia*. (Author's Collection)

The *Marconi* at Hobart, Tasmania. (Tim Noble Collection)

Clockwise from left: Italian Line super ships together at Genoa (ALF Collection); the giant *Michelangelo* (left) and *Raffaello* at Genoa (ALF Collection) New York's Pier 86 in August 1973: the *Michelangelo* is on the left, the *Raffaello* on the right. (Author's Collection)

The *Michelangelo* was seriously damaged in an Atlantic storm during an April 1966 westbound crossing to New York. (ALF Collection)

The *Enrico C* was the former French *Provence*. (ALF Collection)

A 'cousin' to the *Andrea Doria*, the 20,500-ton *Federico C* was completed in 1958 as the first new build for Costa Line. (ALF Collection)

The *Columbus C* (the former *Kungsholm* of 1953) sank at her Cádiz berth as shown here in August 1984. P&O's *Sea Princess* (ex-*Kungsholm* of 1966) is on the right. (Author's Collection)

The ex-*Enrico C* as the *Symphony* being scrapped on the beaches of Alang in India in 2001. (ALF Collection)

Modern Costa cruising: the 112,000grt Costa Concordia. (Costa Cruises)

MSC's Monterey continued to wear her American colours on the bow. (Luis Miguel Correia Collection)

MSC cruising: the mighty MSC Fantasia. (MSC Cruises)

Cruising future: the 154,000-ton, 4,140-passenger MSC Seaside, due in 2016. (MSC Cruises)

A 1930s-style poster promoting the Lido Route, or 'the Sunny Southern Route' as it was also called, to Europe. (Norman Knebel Collection)

Italian Line to South America: a sailing schedule from the 1950s. (Norman Knebel Collection)

The first voyages of the *Giulio Cesare* in 1951. (Norman Knebel Collection)

Italian Line's Latin American passenger services. (Norman Knebel Collection)

Adriatica Line service from Venice to Istanbul. (Norman Knebel Collection)

The introduction of the new *Esperia* in 1949. (Norman Knebel Collection)

The Hellenic Mediterranean Lines sailed eastern Mediterranean waters. (Norman Knebel Collection)

Typaldos Lines amassed a large passenger fleet in the 1960s, but disappeared in bankruptcy in 1968. (Norman Knebel Collection)

The combo ship *Israel* and her sister *Zion* maintained the Haifa–New York run. (Norman Knebel Collection)

Costa cruise fleet in the 1970s. (Author's Collection)

Lloyd Triestino to Australia in the 1950s. (Norman Knebel Collection)

A striking brochure cover from the early 1960s. (Author's Collection)

Costa Mediterranean cruising in 1961. (Norman Knebel Collection)

Costa Line poster art in the 1950s. (Norman Knebel Collection)

8

TURKEY

The classic *Ankara* arriving at Naples. (Eric Johnson Collection)

Turkish Maritime Lines: *Ankara*

In the 1950s, the Turkish passenger-ship fleet, although smaller and used mostly in inter-Mediterranean services, numbered as many fourteen passenger vessels. They belonged to the Turkish Maritime Lines. The 9,400grt *Tarsus*, the former American Export Lines' combination passenger-cargo ship *Exochorda*, dating from 1931, was considered the flagship. Apart from voyages between Istanbul and other Mediterranean ports, she made occasional Atlantic crossings to New York and, in 1960, was on charter to the short-lived Fiesta Cruise Lines for a series of seven-night New York–Bermuda sailings. Other ships included the *Akdeniz*, *Karadeniz, Iskenderun* and *Samsun*. Another was a pioneer for educational and lecture-themed cruises, the 6,178grt, 375-passenger *Ankara*. She sailed for extended periods under charter for Britain's Swan Hellenic Cruises, a London-based specialty cruise operator that later became part of P&O.

Like her Turkish fleet mates *Tarsus*, *Adana* and *Istanbul*, the 409ft-long *Ankara* was formerly American, having been built in 1927 as the *Iroquois* for the coastal services – between New York, Jacksonville and Miami, and occasional cruises – of the Clyde-Mallory Lines. Used during the Second World War as the hospital ship USS *Solace*, she was not restored for US flag passenger service, but instead sold to the Turks in 1948. Used initially on the extended Istanbul–Mediterranean–Marseilles service, she offered everything from deluxe staterooms with full bath and sitting room to eight-bunk dormitories. She began cruising for Swan in the 1960s and continued for over a decade, until she was decommissioned in 1977 and then scrapped five years later. Despite being older and with fewer amenities than many other ships, she was a great favourite for a select segment of the British cruise market. Her guest lecturers and well planned itineraries, often with historic stops, were her selling points.

Demolition at Aliaga in Turkey – the *Ankara* on the left, the *Iskenderun*, also Turkish, on the right. This photo is dated 1982. (Steffen Weirauch)

Sue Mauger joined Swan in 1966 and was soon assigned to duties as a cruise assistant aboard the *Ankara*. She later recalled:

We were of course a chartered ship and so there were Turkish officers and crew with a British cruise staff. Mr Swan, the son of the founder, went on most of the cruises, which were usually fourteen days in length. We touched lots of smaller, more remote ports – often tendering the passengers ashore. There would be about 300 passengers and the ship was generally sold-out solid. As part of the London-based staff, we were given cabins in the bow, four-berth rooms in the very front of the ship. We were among the first to regularly go into the Black Sea, to tightly controlled Soviet ports like Odessa and Yalta. There were days of paperwork for documentation – and everything had to be done in duplicates. But we were always cleared immediately. I remember that the Chandris cruise ships sometimes had to wait for hours.

'The passengers were almost all intellectual types,' added Mrs Mauger:

Among them were some great characters. They were, however, all people who loved history. Occasionally we had informal picnics on a beach, but mostly there were intensive excursions ashore. There was no entertainment except a pianist in the evenings. On sea days, there were three or four talks in daytime and then an after-dinner speaker. Sir Mortimer Wheeler, a very well known British archaeologist, was a guest lecturer at least three times a year. His cruises were fully booked a year in advance. We also had the Archbishop of Canterbury on occasion. The list of speakers' credentials was most impressive – Oxford, Cambridge, Edinburgh University. The talks were given in great detail and were attended regularly.

'The old *Ankara* steamed about,' concluded Sue Mauger. 'It was actually rather primitive on the inside. She had very few cabins with private bathrooms, but mostly ones only with washbasins. Public toilets and showers were along the corridors. But it did not seem to matter. She was always a very, very popular ship.'

The *Ankara* was later replaced (and scrapped in 1982) by another chartered ship, Epirotiki Lines' *Orpheus*, for some years. Swan had their own ship, the *Minerva*, beginning in 1995.

Interior views of the *Ankara*. (Andrew Kilk Collection)

OTHER FLAGS

Khedivial Mail Line: *Khedive Ismail* & *Mohamed Ali El-Kebir*

After we met on a luxury cruise in the 1990s, Marion Carlson recalled her very first voyage:

> My first sea journey was on a small combination passenger-cargo ship, a converted vessel, with very limited amenities. In 1949, I sailed from Hoboken, New Jersey to Alexandria, Egypt. It was a six-week trip altogether aboard a small Egyptian passenger ship, the *Khedive Ismail*. There were about seventy-five passengers aboard, some Italians, some Egyptians and some Americans going on Mediterranean and Egyptian tours.

Built during the Second World War as Victory ships, the 7,600grt *Khedive Ismail* (the former *United Victory*) and her sister ship the *Mohamed Ali El-Kebir*, were sold to the Alexandria-based Khedivial Mail Line in 1947 and rebuilt with extended quarters for up to 100 passengers, all in one class. Essentially cargo-carrying ships, these 17-knot vessels ran a monthly service of sorts, from New York, Philadelphia, Baltimore and Norfolk across to varied Mediterranean ports such as Lisbon, Barcelona, Marseilles, Genoa, Naples, Piraeus and, of course, Alexandria. Later, their itineraries were extended through to Suez to Karachi and Bombay. The fare to Alexandria from New York, a voyage sometimes as long as three weeks, was about $250 by the mid 1950s.

'The *Khedive Ismail* had very plain interiors. Not much had been done from her days as a wartime transport at the end of the Second World War,' recalled Mrs Carlson:

> There was one lounge and where lectures were given on Mediterranean and Egyptian history. There was, as I remember, a very steep stairwell down to the dining room, but the food was forgettable. It was fried potatoes morning, noon and night! The stewards were very generous with the leftovers. They gave it

to the poor at Marseilles and at Naples. There were so many very, very poor people in southern Europe, in the Mediterranean, in the late 1940s. I recall seeing hundreds of barefoot children lining the docksides in various ports.

While the officers and deck crews were Egyptian, some of the passenger stewards and waiters were Italians, left over from the famous Italian Line and out of work in the late 1940s. Several had been used to far grander settings, however, having served aboard the likes of Mussolini's super liners *Rex* and *Conte di Savoia*. 'We did have two special passengers aboard our sailing,' concluded Mrs Carlson. 'King Farouk's two sisters were aboard and, before we actually docked, they were taken ashore in Alexandria harbour by the Royal Chris Craft.'

The 455ft-long *Khedive Ismail* was renamed *Cleopatra* in 1956. The New York passenger services for *Cleopatra* and *Mohamed Ali El-Kebir* ended by 1960, however. For a short time, both ships ran a service between eastern Canada, the Great Lakes and the Mediterranean, marketed as the Canada-Orient Line. They were later downgraded to pure freighters and finally to tramp steamers working odd charters. Both ships, well worn and tired, were later scrapped.

Jadrolinija: *Dalmatia* & *Istra*

After the Second World War, Yugoslavia ran several combination passenger-cargo ships – namely the sixty-passenger *Hrvatska* (a converted Victory ship) and the forty-four-berth *Srbija* – on the Rijeka–Mediterranean–US East Coast run. In 1965, two 5,700grt ships, the *Dalmatia* and *Istra*, were constructed in home waters at Pula. They were used initially on the Rijeka–eastern Mediterranean run and later cruising, but have long since been sold off. The *Dalmatia* was scrapped while the *Istra* went on to become the *Astra*, *Astra I*, *Arion* and was still about in 2015 as the Portuguese-owned *Porto*.

NEW BUILDS OF THE 1960S

Italian Line: *Leonardo da Vinci*

'The *Leonardo da Vinci*, built to replace the sunken *Andrea Doria*, was the Italian sensation of the early 1960s,' recalled John Palermo:

She was the ultimate Italian liner then – and everyone, it seemed, wanted to sail in her. She had very modern as well as luxurious public rooms, better cabins and no less than six pools – three for adults, three for kids. The first-class pool could be heated with infrared lamps. There was closed-circuit television, gala buffets in the evening and hand-picked officers and crew.

Once we sailed over on the new *Da Vinci* and then returned on the elderly *Vulcania*. There was about 35 years in age between the two ships, but it felt like a century. But soon, we, like many others, switched over to the airlines, to the speed of the jets. We really didn't want to, but there was no choice – it was hours compared to days! Sadly, I never again sailed to the Mediterranean on the great Italian Line. But those ocean liner crossings remain strong, cherished memories. I still have postcards of each of the Italian liners.

Captain Raffaelle Gavino's first love among the Italian Line ships might just have been the *Leonardo da Vinci*. He spent ten years on that 1,348-passenger ship, sailing on transatlantic crossings and on her special long winter cruises, such as the annual six-week 'Cradle of the World' voyages that toured the Mediterranean from end to end. 'The *da Vinci* was really a floating museum,' he nostalgically recalled. 'She was an ambassador of Italian art and culture with great rooms decorated with paintings and sculptures and tapestries. We often carried celebrities on board: President Tito of Yugoslavia, Paul Newman, Gloria Swanson, Zachary Scott, Joan Fontaine, Renata Tebaldi and the King of Morocco.'

After some reassignments to such other passenger ships like the *Rossini* and *Verdi* as well as some Italian Line freighters, Captain Gavino returned to the *Leonardo da Vinci* for her final voyages. 'She made a special cruise from Genoa to the North Cape and northern European cities in the summer of 1975 and then made the final New York–Genoa crossing for the Italian Line in June 1976,' he noted. 'I was also master in 1977–78 when she sailed for ICI (Italian Cruises International) on three- and four-day cruises between Port Everglades, Nassau and Freeport. But these were unsuccessful. She was a very expensive ship to operate.'

The *Leonardo da Vinci* under construction at Genoa in 1958. (Gillespie-Faber Collection)

The 761ft-long *Leonardo da Vinci* fitting out at the Ansaldo yard in the spring of 1960. (Italian Line)

Nightfall at Genoa: from left to right: the *Rhodesia Castle*, the freighter *President Jackson* and the *Leonardo da Vinci*. (Italian Line)

Summer morning: the 33,340grt liner arrives in New York for the first time in July 1960. (Moran Towing & Transportation Co.)

Gala maiden departure from Genoa for the 23-knot *Leonardo da Vinci*. (ALF Collection)

Clockwise from above: the imposing bow of the 1,326-passenger *da Vinci* (Italian Line); high modernity: first class aboard the *Leonardo da Vinci* (Italian Line); contemporary styling aboard the *da Vinci*. (Italian Line)

After dark: the tourist-class lido deck. (Italian Line)

Departing from Naples. (Gillespie-Faber Collection)

Maiden arrival at New York's Pier 84. (Moran Towing & Transportation Co.)

Goddess in ruins: the capsized *Leonardo da Vinci* at La Spezia in the late summer of 1980. (Antonio Scrimali)

Righted and prepared for final scrapping, the *Leonardo da Vinci* at the end of her days in 1981. (Antonio Scrimali)

Winter morning at New York: from left to right: the *Bremen*, *Leonardo da Vinci* and *Cristoforo Colombo*. (Sal Scannella Collection)

Lloyd Triestino: *Galileo Galilei* & *Guglielmo Marconi*

The *Guglielmo Marconi* was not especially well known in North American travel circles at least until the late 1970s. And then it was just a spark – gone in a flash, as they say. The strong Italian unions pressed the government ministries in Rome to continue to run passenger liners even after most of their fleet had run up huge losses while carrying fractional amounts of passengers and then been abruptly retired. The Italian Line itself pulled the plug by 1977, for example. The government responded, at least very briefly, with ICI – a newly formed company called Italian Cruises International. With little in the way of refitting, modernisation or even preparation for the demanding US cruise trade, they took the 27,000grt *Guglielmo Marconi*, dubbed simply as *Marconi* for advertising and sales purposes, and placed her on the New York–Caribbean cruise run in December 1978. It could not have been less successful. The ship repeatedly failed its important US public health inspections. By the following June, the ship was laid up, awaiting yet another role. In the winter of 2001, the ship sailed off to the breakers after a rather interesting thirty-eight-year career.

Trieste-based Lloyd Triestino was second only to the great Italian Line for passenger ships under national colours. It was definitely older, dating from 1837, whereas Italian Line was a creation through mergers inspired by the Mussolini government in 1932. Lloyd Triestino also served more exotic ports: the eastern Mediterranean, the Middle and Far East, Australia, and South and East Africa. Before the Second World War, their most famous passenger ship was the *Victoria*, one of the fastest, most advanced motor liners of the 1930s.

In the early 1950s, the company built three sets of brand-new passenger-cargo liners: the *Australia*, *Neptunia* and *Oceania* for the run from Genoa and Naples via Suez to Melbourne and Sydney; the *Asia* and *Victoria* to such ports as Bombay, Singapore and Hong Kong; and finally, the *Africa* and *Europa* bound for the likes of Mombasa, Durban and Cape Town. They carried merchants, businessmen and their families, the clergy, a few tourists and lots of migrants, especially on the Australian service. That route had the most promise and, since in the early 1960s competitor shipowners such as P&O-Orient, Lauro, Sitmar, Cogedar and Chandris were adding new liners, Lloyd Triestino needed to reaffirm its presence down under as well. And so, with lots of Italian government lire in hand, the company built a pair of large, fast, very modern and generally very comfortable sisters, the 705ft-long *Galileo Gaililei* and *Guglielmo Marconi*. Completed in 1963, they were the quickest Italian liners to Australian ports: twenty-three days from Genoa to Sydney. They were also among the most modern. Initially, they were to be fitted with lattice-style funnels, but Lloyd Triestino passed on that idea and instead they were used on the new, far bigger Italian liners *Michelangelo* and *Raffaello*.

The three-class *Australia* and her sisters *Neptunia* and *Oceania* of Lloyd Triestino were popular on the Italy–Australia run. (ALF Collection)

The sisters *Asia* and *Victoria* (seen here) looked after the Italy–Far East run. (Lloyd Triestino)

The *Australia, Neptunia* and *Oceania* later became Italian Line's 'Three Musicians' – *Donizetti, Rossini* and *Verdi.* (Italian Line)

The sisters *Guglielmo Marconi* (seen here) and *Galileo Galilei* were 1960s sensations on the Europe–Australia run. (ALF Collection)

Lloyd Triestino fleet mates: the *Guglielmo Marconi* and the *Europa* together at Las Palmas. (ALF Collection)

Modern comfort: the theatre aboard the *Galileo Galilei*. (Maurizio Eliseo Collection)

With 1,700 berths on board, some 1,500 were in low-fare tourist class. This was heavily supported not only by Italian, but Greek and even some Middle Eastern migrants. 'Arguments and even fighting were common among these migrants, who were worried and often tense after leaving their homelands and heading for the unknown of Australian life,' reported a former staff member. 'We had a sort of police staff in tourist class and once we even had to use tranquiliser guns to calm things. Many of the migrants were very poor village people, who knew little of other ways of the world. On board, there were lots of ethnic and cultural differences.'

The migrant trade fell away by the early 1970s, however. Migrants were now going on cheap air flights instead. The two struggling liners were placed on around-the-world itineraries in hopes of getting a few more guests. But very few booked. By 1976–77, the 23-knot *Marconi* was temporarily swung over to the Italian Line for use on the Genoa–Rio–Buenos Aires run as a companion to the *Cristoforo Colombo*, while the *Galileo* was chartered to Chandris Cruises, the Greek cruise line. There was talk that both would be bought completely by the ever-expanding Chandris firm. Instead, only the *Galileo* went, becoming a Panama-flag cruise ship, often for New York and US East Coast-based service. The *Marconi* was finally sold to another Italian company, Costa Cruises, which had her rebuilt as its *Costa Riviera*.

The highly modernised 850-passenger all-first class *Costa Riviera* seemed to divide her time: the Caribbean out of Port Everglades in winter, the Mediterranean from Genoa in summer. She had a brief turn in 1993–94 as the *American Adventurer* for the short-lived American Family Cruises before reverting to direct Costa operation. 'She was old, less colourful, perhaps dated,' said the late Robert Pelletier, following a Canary Islands cruise aboard her in the late 1990s. 'I enjoyed her, but you could see she no longer matched the new, high-tech, glitzy likes of, say, the 85,000-ton *Costa Atlantica*. The *Costa Riviera* was reduced to offering discount cruises, a sort of lost child within the fleet.'

The *Galileo* was extensively rebuilt in 1990, becoming the *Meridian* for a new, more luxurious Chandris division, Celebrity Cruises. Thereafter she ran seasonal, spring–autumn seven-day cruises between New York and Bermuda and then spent the remaining months in the Caribbean on cruises from Port Everglades. She was about to embark on a series of six- and eight-week cruises in the fall of 1997 when Singapore-based Sun Cruises offered an astounding $62 million for the 34-year-old ship. Quickly, she became their *Sun Vista* for Southeast Asian cruising. But her days were numbered – on 21 May 1999, she burned out and then sank off the Malaysian coast.

The *Costa Riviera*, the former *Marconi*, resumed European cruises for Costa until sold for scrap in India in 2001.

Even Lloyd Triestino was gone by then – the much diminished company had been sold in 1998 to Taiwan's Evergreen Line, a huge container ship company.

Zim Lines: *Shalom*

The growth of the Israeli merchant marine was highlighted in the early 1960s with the *Shalom*, a 25,500-tonner built at Saint-Nazaire in France and aimed at greatly enhancing the Haifa–New York service. She was built as part of West German reparations. The 629ft-long *Shalom* received a joyous reception when commissioned in April 1964, but was in fact a great financial disappointment. She was sold off in 1967 and became, in succession, the *Hanseatic*, *Doric*, *Royal Odyssey* and *Regent Sun*. Laid up in 1995, she was to have been revived as the *Sun*, but this never came to pass and instead the ship was sold to Indian scrappers. She sank en route to India, however, on 26 July 2001 while off the South African coast.

Italian Line: *Michelangelo & Raffaello*

'The *Michelangelo* and *Raffaello* often used to pass one another at sea, in mid-Atlantic, and this always caused lots of excitement,' recalled Giancarlo Roccatagliata, a one-time maître'd aboard those ships. 'There would be horns blowing and balloons and flares and, of course, lots of waving. It was a great show. The ships would be traveling in opposite directions at combined speeds of well over 50 knots!'

Completed in 1965, the 45,900-ton ships were built – the *Michelangelo* at Ansaldo's Genoa-Sestri yards, the *Raffaello* at Cantieri Riuniti dell'Adriatico at San Marco, near Trieste – for Italian Line's express service between Naples, Genoa, Cannes, Algeciras and New York. So enthused by them, New York City officials even offered to demolish some old railroad piers just north of Luxury Liner Row at West 66th Street and build a new passenger ship terminal just for the Italian Line. A square facility with three berths similar to Holland America's new Pier 40 at West Houston Street, an artist rendering referred to the project as 'Italian Line's Pier 99'. In fact, beginning in late 1963, the Italian Line took over the lease on Cunard's 1,100ft-long Pier 90 at West 50th Street, which had been built especially in 1936 for the *Queen Mary* and *Queen Elizabeth*. And so, these sleek, new Italian beauties with their long white hulls, raked bows and birdcage-like stacks used Pier 90.

The *Shalom* arriving in New York in a photograph dated June 1964. (Gillespie-Faber Collection)

Modernised especially with a new funnel, the former *Shalom* is seen here in a later guise, as the *Regent Sun*. (Alan Goldfinger Collection)

The artist rendering of the *Michelangelo* and *Raffaello* as released in 1963. The first rendering, however, showed a black hull for both super liners. (Italian Line)

Bon voyage: the *Raffaello* departing from New York's Pier 90. (ALF Collection)

Maiden arrival for the *Raffaello* in August 1965. The *Michelangelo* and *United States* are in the background. (Italian Line)

'These sister ships were actually already too late for the declining transatlantic trade of the second half of the 1960s,' noted Roccatagliata:

The Italian government actually had to build them under pressure from several powerful Italian unions. They gave work to the shipyards, to the dockers and especially to the seamen. At first, they were planned as smaller ships, at 35,000 tons each and so just a little bigger than the *Leonardo da Vinci*. But early construction was stopped and the plans changed for bigger, longer liners. They were great ships in many ways, but not financially. They never earned a single *lire*, even as cruise ships, with 700 or so berths in tourist class, because the cabins were too small and too austere. This too cut into their possible profits, making them big white elephants.

'The government-owned Italian Line never had a post-war liner that was ideally suited to cruising,' added Roccatagliata:

All of them were traditionally class-divided ships that were not easily convertible on all-one-class cruise ships. Apart from one- and two-week cruises, we tried longer cruises as well – Carnival in Rio, the Black Sea & Holy Land and up to Norway and the North Cape. I remember one North Cape trip when we only had ten Americans and 600 Italians on board.

The *Michelangelo* and *Raffaello* sailed for only ten years. In the very end, they and other Italian Line passenger ships were plagued with an added problem: strikes. 'There were lots of strikes, beginning in the early '70s, and sometimes for short but disruptive twenty-four and forty-eight hours – and too many of them for any silly reason,' concluded Giancarlo Roccatagliata. 'Once there was a strike simply because the ship ran out of mineral water for the crew. In the end, between 1975 and 1977, the unions and all their all-too-obedient members pushed the Italian Line and the government to close out all passenger ship services.'

'Rome suddenly cut almost all passenger liner subsidies in 1975,' added Captain Piovino:

There was also a tremendous decline in passengers and very expensive fuel oil prices. Ships like the *Michelangelo* and *Raffaello* were losing huge amounts of money. The ships were withdrawn and thousands were suddenly out of work. Many staff went into early retirement while others went to cargo ships. Lots of Italian Line personnel found jobs with Sitmar, Costa, Princess, Home Lines and Carnival Cruise Lines. Alone, seven former Italian Line captains joined Carnival.

Clockwise from right: Isolation: seen in this 1977 photograph, the faded, rusting *Michelangelo* in Iran. (William Fox); noontime departure for the *Michelangelo*; the *Bremen* is on the far right. (Italian Line); the 902ft-long *Michelangelo* in her maiden year. (Italian Line)

Captain Piovino went on to become master of Carnival's first three liners: *Mardi Gras*, *Carnivale* and *Festivale*.

Captain Fossati was assigned to the decommissioning of the *Michelangelo* and *Raffaello*:

They were actually kept in service until the very last moment. After their final crossings [the *Raffaello* in April 1975, the *Michelangelo* three months later], we kept them at Genoa for a few months and then, in September, moved them to Porto Venere in the Gulf of La Spezia. We moored them side-by-side, but in reverse. This gave them double anchors at each end. On board, everything stripped. A crew of fifty moved all the art, carpets, even the china and glassware ashore and then to warehouses. We were instructed, however, to especially leave all the instruments on the bridge.

Stripping these Italian liners had become a rather familiar practice. Because they were state-owned ships, their passenger fittings – particularly their artworks – found their way ashore and into government, state-owned businesses and even the homes of government ministers and officials. Art from the *Giulio Cesare*, for example, was divided up and some went to a Milanese bank. Pieces from the *Leonardo da Vinci* later found their way into various government offices in Rome. Smaller items, however, were placed in the basements of the Italian Line's Genoa headquarters until, in the mid 1980s, that property was closed and sold off. Unfortunately, this archive finished up in government incinerators.

Rino Rivieccio, one-time purser aboard both the *Michelangelo* and *Raffaello*, went aboard the two giant Italian liners in the fall of 1975. 'It was like seeing a person dying,' he remembered:

> Only a watchman was aboard. There were very few lights. On deck, there were nets over the swimming pools. It was all very quiet – not a sound. It was haunting. There weren't even flags at the masts. There were rumours at the time that the 10-year-old ships would soon be scrapped on the beaches of La Spezia.

While it was also rumoured that a Liechtenstein-based organisation wanted to make them over as floating cancer research, treatment and recovery clinics while running two and three Mediterranean cruises, other companies inspected the legendary pair. Costa Line thought they would be too expensive to operate and so did Norwegian Caribbean Lines. Chandris Lines was interested, but then became more concerned about the decline of its Europe–Australia migrant trade and just could not see them as full-time cruise ships. Home Lines was very interested, but their bids were rejected in the end by the Italian government. The Soviets also had a look and so did C.Y. Tung, and there was a Brazilian firm that wanted them but for low-cost housing at Santos. It was the Iranians, however, who got the pair in the end.

In an oil-swap deal with Italy, the Shah of Iran's government took them for use as military barracks. They passed through the Suez Canal to their new homes in 1977 – the *Michelangelo* to Bandar Abbas, the *Raffaello* to Bushehr. Afterwards army officers, troops and young cadets piled aboard. There was, however, a rather lengthy plan drawn up in 1978 that would see them refitted and restyled as luxury cruise ships. While Iranian-owned, they would use a flag of convenience and sail Mediterranean as well as Caribbean waters with reduced capacities of 1,300 each. They were to be renamed *Reza Shah the Great* and *Cyrus the Great*. These plans never materialised, however.

In 1978, Captain Fossati went to Iran as part of a cooperative arrangement between Italy and Iran. 'There were fifty Italians on board each ship for maintenance as well as advisory purposes,' he recalled. 'But already, the ships were in very, very poor condition. It was clear they could never sail again.' While they also housed American technicians working in Iran on oil company contracts, the ships fell further and further into disrepair. Their hulls gathered more and more rust, the outer decks began to buckle and – worst of all – they were invaded by armies of rats.

The future for the two liners was bleak. In February 1983, the *Raffaello* was bombed and then sunk during an Iraqi air attack on Bushehr. Her remains barely poked above the harbour waters. Four years later, on 4 February 1987, the 9,200-ton freighter *Iran Salam* went aground at Bushehr and was badly damaged. This incident would have been quite ordinary, in fact almost unnoticed, except that the ship grounded on the sunken wreckage of the *Raffaello*. Later reports that the *Raffaello* was to be salvaged never came to pass.

Meanwhile, the *Michelangelo* lingered on, caught in veils of both mystery and rumour. She was to have been sold to Florida-based Premier Cruise Lines for short cruise service to the Bahamas and then it was reported that she was to be scrapped at Kaohsiung on Taiwan in 1988. Both reports proved false. She was, however, finally sold to Pakistani scrap merchants in the summer of 1991.

The former pride of the Italian fleet, at 26 years old the *Michelangelo* was a sad, very rusted, almost unrecognisable sight as she arrived under tow at Gadani Beach in July 1991. She was the biggest liner yet dismantled in that otherwise remote port. By the following winter, all that remained was her double bottom.

In 2000, Costa Cruises acquired the huge model of the *Michelangelo* that once graced the Milan railway station and placed it aboard their refurbished, enlarged cruise ship *Costa Classica*.

Home Lines: *Oceanic*

'She was a most important ship, one of the very finest ever and, in her time, the high-point of the great success of the Home Lines,' according to Captain Mario Vespa, a company vice president. 'We designed her to do as much as 27 knots on the North Atlantic, to do Southampton to Québec City in five days flat. But then, of course, the *Oceanic* became the greatest, most successful cruise ship of her time.'

Built by Cantieri Riuniti dell'Adriatico at Monfalcone and practically alongside the larger *Raffaello* and then the *Eugenio C*, Home had ordered the 1,600-passenger ship in 1960 for the final era of North Atlantic passenger service. It was planned that she would be the finest liner on the Canadian run, sailing between Cuxhaven (Hamburg), Le Havre, Southampton over to Québec City and Montréal for about eight months of the year. In deep winter, she would cruise from New York to the Caribbean. But by the fall of 1963, Home Lines realised Atlantic bookings were declining and so decided on year-round cruising – weekly Saturday sailings on seven-day cruises to Nassau. Such full-time cruising and with such a large liner was a gamble.

In the end, the success of the *Oceanic* was beyond the wildest expectations of the Home Lines. In her first season, with minimum fares beginning at $175, she was booked to 98 per cent capacity. While she ran her weekly cruises to the Bahamas between April and December, she went on longer Caribbean cruises (ten to twenty-one days) in deep winter. Her capacity was then specially reduced from 1,200 on the Nassau to a more intimate 800. 'These cruises were far more formal,' remembered Len Chapman, a junior purser with Home Lines in the 1970s. 'It was all top-shelf. We provided the very best service. We had "night stewards", for example – elderly, highly trained gentlemen who had been with Home Lines for over twenty years. The Italian service and especially the cuisine were legendary.'

Although there were rumours about in 1986 that the *Oceanic* might be sold to Chandris-Fantasy Cruises, she was bought in the end by Florida-headquartered Premier Cruise Lines and marketed as the *Starship Oceanic*. After Premier collapsed into bankruptcy in 2000, the ship was sold to Spain's Pullmanturs, reverted to the name *Oceanic* and ran Mediterranean as well as South American cruises. Sold again in 2009, this time to Japan's Peace Boat Organisation, she began making educational world cruises. The 47-year-old ship sailed only for another two years, however, before being sold to Chinese buyers for scrap.

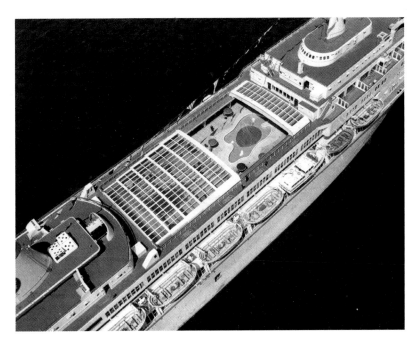

The midship's lido deck aboard the 774ft long *Oceanic* with its unique glass ceiling. (Gillespie-Faber Collection)

Busy Saturday morning at New York in June 1975. From from left to right: *Sagafjord, Doric, Michelangelo, Oceanic, Rotterdam* and *Statendam*. (Port Authority of New York & New Jersey)

Gala reception: the maiden arrival of the innovative *Oceanic* at New York in April 1965. (Gillespie-Faber Collection)

11

COSTA

Costa Line: *Eugenio C*

When I visited the Lloydwerft shipyard at Bremerhaven in the autumn of 1995 to research the building of the 75,000-ton *Costa Victoria* for a commemorative book, there were brief rumours that Costa Cruises' older but much beloved and still popular *Eugenio C* would be gutted, re-engined, modernised and restyled purposely for longer luxury cruises. Her classic 1960s exterior was to be retained, however. Nearly 30 years old, the 30,500grt ship was, in fact, then owned by the Bremer-Vulkan Group, the financially troubled parent of Lloydwerft. Costa had 'traded' the 712ft-long *Eugenio Costa* to the German industrial giant as a down payment for the intended 78,000-ton *Costa Olympia*, a near-sister to the *Costa Victoria*. But plans for the older, steam-turbine-driven and therefore costly to operate ship went astray soon afterward. She was dropped from Costa's 1997 cruise schedules and then, in February 1998, she was sold to British buyers, a shipping group called Lowline. It was the end of the Italian/Costa chapter, for that remarkable ship.

Genoa-based Costa, which had freighters, went into the passenger ship business, prompted largely by the post-war boom in migrant traffic, in 1948. There were as many as 100 family members working in the company by 1980, but Giacomo Costa's business started out as an edible oil concern in 1860. In 1924, his three sons diversified in shipping, small freighters transporting Costa oils. After the Second World War, in 1947–48 larger ships joined the fleet including the decommissioned British troopship *Southern Prince*. She became Costa's first passenger ship, the renamed *Anna C*, and, after refitting, set off from Genoa on 30 March 1948. A 12,000-tonner, she was refitted to carry 1,001 passengers – mostly migrants, refugees and displaced persons from Naples and Genoa to 'new lives' after landing in Rio de Janeiro, Santos, Montevideo and Buenos Aires. While not a large passenger ship, she was quick to establish a strong reputation. Her levels of comfort, overall shipboard style and even the standards of her kitchens were highly recognised. Furthermore, the 524ft-long *Anna C* was distinctive: she was Italy's first air-conditioned passenger ship.

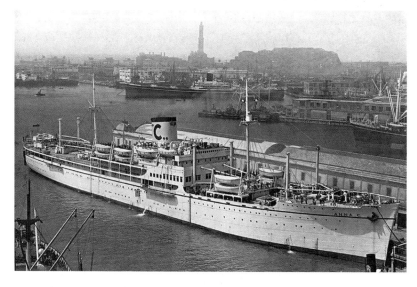

Costa's first passenger ship, the 11,000-ton *Anna C*, at Genoa. (Costa Line)

The 17,000grt *Bianca C* was one of Costa's short-lived passenger ships. She joined the company in 1960, only to burn in the Caribbean, at Grenada, two years later. (Costa Line)

1960s style: a bar-lounge aboard the *Enrico C*. (Paolo Piccione Collection)

A bar aboard the 1966-built *Eugenio C*. (Paolo Piccione Collection)

During a special cruise visit, the handsome *Eugenio C* departs from New York in this 1978 view. (Alan Goldfinger Collection)

Costa soon looked to more second-hand passenger tonnage and commissioned its first new build, the 20,400-ton *Federico C,* in 1958. The *Anna C* endured until 1971.

By the mid 1960s, the stunning *Eugenio C* was the culmination of Costa's traditional passenger ship business. She was the very last class-divided liner used in port-to-port service before the great transition to the cruise generation began in the 1970s. 'What the classically beautiful *Rotterdam* was to the Holland America Line and her loyal followers, the *Eugenio C* [renamed *Eugenio Costa* in 1987] was to Costa and many, many travellers. She was a favoured, much loved ship,' noted Paolo Piccione, a Genoa-based naval architect who had worked closely with Costa and its passenger ships:

The *Eugenio C* is a classic ship, built in a different era, the 1960s, and for a different trade. She was an 'ocean liner'. She was also a cousin in ways to the superb *Oceanic* of Home Lines. They two ships were, of course, built at the same shipbuilder – Cantieri Riuniti dell'Adriatico [later renamed Fincantieri].

The early 1960s was a golden age of superb liners in Italian shipbuilding: the *Leonardo da Vinci* in 1960, the *Guglielmo Marconi* and *Galileo Galilei* in 1963, and then the *Michelangelo*, *Raffaello* and aforementioned *Oceanic* two years later. The twin-screw *Eugenio C* had her debut in August 1966. Built at Monfalcone near Venice, the fast, 27-knot ship was designed especially for one of the last great ocean liner services: Europe to South America. She sailed on a monthly schedule between Genoa, Cannes, Barcelona and Lisbon

Small and sleek: the long-lived *Franca C*. (Alex Duncan)

to Rio de Janeiro, Santos, Montevideo and Buenos Aires. Well suited to that trade in those otherwise airline-dominated days, she carried as many as 1,636 passengers in three classes – 178 in first class, 356 in cabin class and 1,102 in tourist. She was, in fact, the last three-class ever built.

Every summer, in August, the peak Italian vacation and therefore cruise period, the *Eugenio C* would become all one class and make a month-long cruise from Genoa. In 1977, for example, she visited New York and other US East Coast ports for the first time. Other trips took her to the Caribbean, the North Cape and Norwegian fjords, the Baltic and around the British Isles. She also visited the St Lawrence region and called at Montréal and Québec City.

By the late 1980s, the old South American liner route was all but finished completely. Like all Costa liners, the *Eugenio Costa* was now cruising full time – around the Mediterranean and occasionally into the Black Sea in summers, and from Rio and Buenos Aires in winter. In 1994, a planned refit and transfer to the short-lived American Family Cruises (a part of the Costa group) as the family-style *American Adventure* was never realised. A Costa fleet mate, the *Costa Riviera*, the former *Guglielmo Marconi* from 1963, sailed but rather briefly as the *American Pioneer*.

Rumours about new 'Mediterranean owners' for the *Eugenio Costa* began circulating in 1996. In fact, she finished her last Costa cruise that November. She was sold to rather unexpected owners, Germany's Bremer Vulcan shipyard (in part exchange for the construction of the new *Costa Victoria*), but then was resold to Lowline Shipping, who in turn chartered the ship to Britain's Direct Cruises for a budget cruise program. Renamed *Edinburgh Castle* (a marketing reminder of the Union-Castle liner of the same name), she was soon troubled with serious mechanical problems. After running some short cruises out of New York as well, both Direct and Lowline went into bankruptcy and the ship itself was auctioned off in 1999 to a creditor – another shipyard in fact, Cammell Laird of Birkenhead.

Cammell Laird promptly chartered the ship to Premier Cruise Lines, renaming her *Big Red Boat III* and giving her a $25 million refit. But in 2000, Premier also collapsed and thereafter Cammell Laird sought another charter before laying up the ship at Freeport in the Bahamas. Eventually sold to a ship management company, who also tried to sell or charter her, the days for the former *Eugenio C* were numbered by 2005. The vessel was sold to Indian scrap merchants, renamed *Big Red* and then sailed via the Azores for the long, slow voyage out to Alang in India and the local scrappers.

12

THE BOOMING CRUISE GENERATION

Costa Cruises

The Costa Line was, for a time in the early 1980s, the largest cruise company in the western world. Only the Soviet passenger fleet of that time was larger. At its peak, Costa operated no less than ten passenger liners. Costa was also one of Italy's largest privately owned companies, with other holdings in cargo shipping, petrochemicals, real estate (particularly in apartment blocks in and around Genoa), newspapers and magazines, and olive oil. In their earlier years in passenger shipping, Costa managed to survive two perils in Italian ship operations: rising labour costs and frequent, disruptive strikes.

By 2015, Costa Cruises (owned by the Carnival Corporation since 2000) was at a peak. It had sixteen cruise ships, used in service throughout the world, and had its largest ships on order (at 168,000 tons and 6,600 passengers). Having previously managing Germany's Aida Cruises and Spain's Iberocruises, Costa itself is currently the biggest cruise operator in Europe.

MSC Cruises

MSC Cruises is an arm of Mediterranean Shipping Company, which, by 2015, was the largest privately owned shipping company in the world. Encompassing cargo ships (mostly large container ships) as well as ferries, MSC's fleet numbered some 425 vessels. These included the world's largest container ship (with a capacity for over 20,000 containers) as well as twelve cruise liners for MSC Cruises. Four new builds are in the works, including a pair of 168,000 tonners for as many as 5,700 passengers each.

MSC first entered the passenger ship business in 1987, operating a single liner, the *Achille Lauro*, under the banner of Star Lauro Cruises. Several second-hand passenger ships followed until the company was renamed MSC Cruises in 1995 and later began building purposeful, brand-new cruise tonnage. In 2015, MSC was listed as the fourth largest cruise operator in the world following Carnival, Royal Caribbean and Norwegian Cruise Lines.

13

LONG-LIVED FORMER ITALIANS

The Former *Augustus*

She was certainly not the last of the Italian liners, but she represented a past era – the era of traditional Mediterranean passenger ships. In 2011, an ocean-going tug towed the former *Augustus* of the Italian Line from Manila in the Philippines to scrappers at Alang in India. Still a very handsome-looking ship, she had endured for sixty years, far longer than any other Italian Line passenger ship and almost longer than any passenger ship with roots in the Mediterranean.

'The *Augustus* was my first ship with the great Italian Line. The year was 1960,' recalled Captain Nicola Arena. Service with big luxury liners between Europe and the United States and also between Europe and South America was still booming. We carried three classes of passengers and we were always full-up.' At the time of our interview, in 1996, the 27,000-ton liner was still in Far Eastern waters, renamed *Asian Princess*, and rumours again surfaced that the ship was to be reactivated for Pacific cruising. Having been laid up for much of the last twenty years, she did little more than move from anchorage at such ports as Hong Kong, Manila, Kaohsiung and Subic Bay. By 1998, she was anchored off the Philippines capital, being looked after by a small caretaker crew. Soon afterwards, to the excitement and interest of ship buffs, there were rumours that the former *Augustus* would be brought back to Genoa and be converted to a moored museum ship, a tribute to the great age of Italian ocean liners. It was at best a very remote idea; nothing came to pass.

As the airlines fully invaded the South Atlantic in the early 1970s, the *Augustus* (and *Giulio Cesare*) lost their trade. The Italian government was also cutting its much needed subsidy to such ships. In addition, fuel oil prices were soaring and the heavily unionised crews demanded pay increases. The *Augustus* made her last trip in January 1976 and then spent some time idle at Naples before being sold to a succession of Eastern owners, most notably the owners of the Philippine President Lines, a big cargo ship operator. She had a succession of names. At first, she was sold to Great Sea & Investment Limited, registered under the flag of the Seychelles and renamed *Great Sea*.

She was moved to Hong Kong, supposedly for repairs and reconditioning. Quickly, frequent rumours began of her being revived as a cruise ship, including sailings from Australia, but nothing materialised. At her moorings, she served at various times as a hotel, conference venue, accommodation ship and maritime training centre.

She was then sold again, in 1980, to Manila-based Ocean King Navigation Company and renamed *Ocean King*. Two years later she was moved from Hong Kong to Manila and later to Subic Bay and, in 1983, she was restyled as the accommodation ship *Philippines* (some reports suggested the spelling *Philipinas*). In 1985, she was renamed yet again, this time as *President*. In 1987, she became the *Asian Princess,* first registered in Hong Kong and then at Manila. She was moved to Keelung but only for further lay up. Exact details and even precise whereabouts became clouded in uncertainty, even mystery. In 1986, several American newspapers including the *New York Times* reported that she was a 'treasure ship' filled with artworks, antiques and other valuable items belonging to ex-President Ferdinand Marcos and his wife Imelda.

Scott Baty, an Australian passenger ship specialist and the author of a book on Pacific liners, visited the former *Augustus* in 1986:

I saw her at Subic Bay, and was invited to have a short private cruise aboard her. She was owned by the Yap family, who also owned the big Philippine President Lines, the country's largest cargo carrier. No one seemed to be sure why they actually bought the ship, but at one point they wanted to start a South Pacific cruise service out of Brisbane with her.

Structurally, she was much the same as originally built, but her passenger quarters had been remodeled in Filipino styles. There seemed to be velvet everywhere – and in reds, oranges and lime green.

At the time of my visit, there were rumors that she might be sold to the Chinese, but this never materialised. Also, it seems that, in the summer of 1983, while she was laid up in Hong Kong harbour, the former *Augustus* was moored alongside one of her former Italian Line fleet mates, the *Cristoforo Colombo*. That ship was soon to be towed across to Taiwan and scrapped.

In 1998, ocean liner expert Peter Knego reported, 'The former *Augustus* is spotless, manned and even raises power on occasion. She has not, however, actually sailed in four years. It will be interesting if she ever sails again.'

The saga of the ex-*Augustus* continued until she was scrapped in India in 2012.

The Former *Franca C*

Shipbuilders could not know but some ships they built go on forever – for decades and decades. Good, solid construction helps but it is probably a matter of fate more than anything else. A prime example, the iconic *QE2* sailed for thirty-nine years, which was longer than any big liner in history. She was also the longest-serving ship in the 175 years of Cunard Line history. And the 70,000-ton *QE2* made other records – she carried more passengers, steamed more miles, visited more ports and made more money than any other super liner in history. A Cunard officer once told me, 'She was innovative, unique, lucky and, most of all, very successful.' These days, however, the *QE2* just waits out in Dubai. After being retired from Cunard service in November 2008, she was to have become a luxury residence, entertainment centre and collection of shops and restaurants, and all while moored on the extravagant Palm Island. Plans did not materialise, however, and then other plans – being a hotel at Cape Town, being berthed in London and, most recently, being used as a moving hotel in Chinese and other Far Eastern ports – failed as well. The fate of the *QE2*, now 46 years old, is uncertain. Another idle liner with an uncertain future, in Philadelphia, is the record-breaking speed queen *United States*. She is 63 years old.

There are other, if less famous, deep-sea passenger ships that endure. The Portuguese-owned *Azores*, still cruising on a British charter, is 67 years old. Completely rebuilt and modernised by the early 1990s, the strong and solid hull dates back to 1948 when the 15,000-ton ship was first commissioned as the Swedish American Line's *Stockholm*. She has had many changes and more than six different names since then. The *Hikawa Maru*, a museum ship at Yokohama, dates from 1930 and the *Rotterdam*, another floating museum (at Rotterdam), was first completed in 1959. Of course, there is the grande dame of all museum and hotel ships, the *Queen Mary*. Moored at Long Beach, near Los Angeles, the last three-funnel ocean liner (and one that crossed the Atlantic 1,000 times and sailed for Cunard for thirty-one years) will turn 80 next year.

But oldest of all of these passenger ships might just be the *Doulos Phos*. In 2015, the little 6,800-ton ship turned 101. And she is a part of current cruising history as well. Back in 1914, the Newport News Shipbuilding & Dry Dock Company in Virginia (where, among others, the super ship *United States* was constructed) launched a small, unnoticed freighter, the *Medina*. Completed on the eve of the First World War, she was built for an American shipowner, the long-gone Mallory Lines, for US inter-coastal freight services. Fortunately, she survived both world wars, but was then to be put up for sale in 1948. Already being over 30 years of age, she might have been scrapped. Instead, she was sold – for a low price – to European shipping operators, but who used a 'flag of convenience' subsidiary, the Panama-flag Compañia Naviera San Miguel. With the pressing post-war need to transport migrants, refugees and displaced persons out of Europe, she was rebuilt as the austere migrant ship *Roma*. Her cargo holds were made over as dormitories, holding as many as 850 at full capacity. An old friend at New York visited the ship soon afterward and described her quarters as being 'close to turn-of-the-century steerage'.

Tens of thousands of Europeans wanted a new post-war life – mostly for economic reasons – and looked to the likes of the United States, Canada, South America, Australia and South Africa for resettlement. Under charter, the *Roma* was sent off on crowded, often cramped voyages, mostly from Genoa and Naples, to Rio de Janeiro and Buenos Aires and, farther afield, to Melbourne and Sydney. In 1950, she was chartered by a religious organisation for cheap travel between New York and the Mediterranean for the special Holy Year celebrations in Rome. The two-week crossings were priced from $110.

In the early 1950s, the Genoa-based Costa Line was beginning to expand its passenger-ship business, begun for them in 1947 and linked to Latin America, and so, in 1952, bought the small, aged *Roma*. Obviously, they saw potential in her robust American hull. She was refitted and improved as the *Franca C*, busily carrying more migrants between Naples, Genoa, Cannes, Barcelona and Lisbon and then across to Rio de Janeiro, Santos, Montevideo and Buenos Aires. Her westward trips were booked to capacity. Costa soon added more passenger ships.

In 1959, despite her 45 years, the 410ft-long *Franca C* was thoroughly rebuilt as a high-standard cruise ship by Costa, upgraded and even re-engined (with new Fiat diesels). In her new guise, she looked sleek, modern and certainly age-defying. Evidently, there was still more life – and profit – in the little ship. Costa sent her off on Mediterranean cruises, to the Adriatic, Greek isles and, on occasion, to the Black Sea and West Africa. She now carried up to 354 passengers, all of them in air-conditioned, brightly coloured, comfortable cabins, and all of them with private bathroom facilities. She had a series of new public rooms, all done in tasteful modern Mediterranean decor, a showroom, dining room and umbrella-lined lido deck complete with kidney-bean-shaped swimming pool.

By the early 1960s, the *Franca C* began to spend her winters at Port Everglades in Florida. Then an infant cruise port, the ship was scheduled for Caribbean cruises from three to fourteen days. A three-night cruise (to Nassau and Freeport) was priced from $59 or less than $20 per person per day. Years later, in 1968, while sailing from San Juan, Puerto Rico, the *Franca C* inaugurated the first air-sea combination sailings. Cruise lines and airlines hereafter became friends. Near the end of her Costa days, in the mid 1970s, the ship was kept closer to home – cruising from Venice to Adriatic and Aegean ports. Almost deservedly, she was laid up in winter and then, in 1977, seemingly out of service forever.

A year later, in 1978, the *Franca C* (then 64) found yet more life – as a floating missionary book and evangelical centre. It was in this role that I visited her as the renamed *Doulos*, registered in Malta but with German owners, at Tenerife in the summer of 1983. She sailed for Operation Mobilisation, created in the 1960s to promote Christian brotherhood and distribute literature. When I visited, the ship had been converted with permanent exhibit space for as many as 4,000 books. Even the outdoor and lido deck were used. Additionally, another 500,000 books were said to be in the ship's holds. The staff of 300 – from the captain to the last assistant cook and greaser – worked as volunteers. The ship sailed the world.

New, strict safety maritime safety regulations finally spelled the end for the *Doulos* (then 95) in 2009. A refit and upgrading would have cost $15 million. In 2010, the *Doulos* was sold to Singapore buyers, who planned to preserve the ship for use at resort on the Indonesian island of Bintan. The plans included installation of restaurants, wine and juice bars, a bookshop, meeting rooms, a maritime museum and, in reflection of her past, a bible school. Nothing has yet materialised, however. The *Doulos* – renamed as the *Doulos Phos* ('Servant of Light') – just waits. Some ships just seem to endure forever.

BIBLIOGRAPHY

Dunn, Laurence. *Passenger Liners*. London, England: Adlard Coles Ltd, 1961.

Dunn, Laurence. *Passenger Liners*. London, England: Adlard Coles Ltd, 1965.

Heine, Frank & Lose, Frank. *Great Passenger Ships of the World*. Hamburg, Germany: Koehlers Verlagsgesellschaft, 2010.

Kludas, Arnold. *Great Passenger Ships of the World: Vol. 4, 1936–50*. Cambridge, England: Patrick Stephens Ltd, 1977.

Kludas, Arnold. *Great Passenger Ships of the World: Vol. 5, 1951–76*. Cambridge, England: Patrick Stephens Ltd, 1977.

Mayes, William. *Cruise Ships* (fifth edition). Windsor, England: Overview Press Ltd, 2014.

Miller, William H. *Great American Passenger Ships*. Stroud, England: The History Press Ltd, 2012.

Miller, William H. *Greek Passenger Liners*. Stroud, England: Tempus Publishing Ltd, 2006.

Miller, William H. *Pictorial Encyclopedia of Ocean Liners, 1860–1994*. Mineola, USA: Dover Publications Inc., 1995.

Official Steamship Guide (1951–63). New York, USA: Transportation Guides, 1964.

Plowman, Peter. *Australian Cruise Ships*. Dural Delivery Centre, New South Wales: Rosenberg Publishing Pty Ltd, 2007.

Plowman, Peter. *Australian Migrant Ships 1946–77*. New South Wales, Australia: Rosenberg Publishing Pty Ltd, 2006.

Plowman, Peter. *Coast to Coast: The Great Australian Coastal Liners*. New South Wales, Australia: Rosenberg Publishing Pty Ltd, 2007.